Study Guide to Accompany
Money, Banking, and the Economy

Third Edition

Study Guide to Accompany

Money, Banking, and the Economy

Thomas Mayer
James S. Duesenberry
Robert Z. Aliber

Third Edition

by
STEVEN BECKMAN
JANET L. WOLCUTT
Wichita State University

W • W • Norton & Company
NEW YORK   LONDON

ISBN 0-393-95559-1

W. W. Norton & Company, Inc., 500 Fifth Avenue, New York, N.Y. 10110
W. W. Norton & Company Ltd., 37 Great Russell Street, London WC1B 3NU

1 2 3 4 5 6 7 8 9 0

Contents

Preface

This study guide is designed to help you understand the material presented in *Money, Banking, and the Economy*, Third Edition, by Thomas Mayer, James S. Duesenberry, and Robert Z. Aliber. Each chapter in the study guide corresponds to one in the text, providing an extensive array of review questions and exercises intended to make you a more active reader. The more time you spend with the textbook and study guide the better, but you will get the maximum benefit from your reading if you approach each chapter in the following way:

1. Read the Learning Objectives and the Key Terms, Concepts, and Institutions. You now know the main points and key terms to watch for as you read the text.

2. Now read the text. Look for the main points in section headings and key terms in boldface type.

3. Try the Self-Tests. These are designed to reinforce what you read and to test your recall of facts and concepts.

4. Take a break. If you try to do more at this point, diminishing returns set in! Do something else, and let your mind absorb what you have learned.

5. Try the Topics for Discussion. This section turns the major points covered in the chapter into questions or applies the points to current situations.

6. The Exercise Questions are the acid test. If you can get the right numerical answer or correctly identify the critical points you are well on your way to mastering the material. These sections are also used to show practical applications, such as how to read bond-market quotations or how to calculate the value of an investment.

7. Some material that we have found helpful for our students has also been included. In Chapter 10, the deposit multipliers are given a closer look in a simple way. In Chapter 17, the key differences between the monetarists and Keynesians are presented in a point-counterpoint format.

Answers are provided at the end of each chapter for the Self-Tests and Exercise Questions, making these parts of the guide largely self-contained. Of course, you will have to read the text to respond to the material in Learning Objectives, Key Terms, and Topics for Discussion. If this study guide helps you to get a better feel for what you understand and what you have to work on, then it has accomplished its purpose. Enjoy your studies!

Steven Beckman
Janet L. Wolcutt

Acknowledgments

We want to thank two teachers who have been important to us, Thomas Mayer of the University of California, Davis, and Edward Kane of Ohio State University. For their help in commenting on the previous edition, we also want to thank E. Dwight Phaup of Union College and, again, Thomas Mayer.

CHAPTER 1　Introduction

Learning Objectives

After studying this chapter, you should be able to

1. understand the importance of money.

2. distinguish between money, wealth and income.

3. explain the three functions of money.

4. understand how a monetary system evolves from a barter system.

5. appreciate the differences between monetary and barter systems.

Key Terms, Concepts, and Institutions

You should be able to define or explain

monetary theory

money

income

standard of value

barter

transaction costs

full-bodied commodity money

credit money

near-money

monetary power

wealth

medium of exchange

store of value

indirect barter

M–1

representative full-bodied money

legal tender

liquidity

Self-Test: Completion

1. Money whose value as a commodity is equal to its value as money is ＿＿＿＿＿.

2. A token that is accepted in exchange only because others will accept it is ＿＿＿＿＿.

3. In the U.S. only ——————— is legal tender.

4. The acceptance of a commodity in trade because it can be traded relatively easily is ———————.

5. Any commodity or concept used to express prices is a ———————.

6. Whatever is routinely accepted in trades is a ———————.

7. ——————— includes items that are highly liquid but are excluded from our money definition.

8. Currency plus checkable deposits can be referred to as ———————.

Self-Test: True-False

1. Cycles in money are the sole cause of business cycles.

2. The evolution of money has been from concrete objects to abstract symbols.

3. Corporate stock is near-money.

4. Credit money has no value.

5. Inflation may result from excessive money growth.

6. Monetary theory is concerned with how the quantity of money and interest rates should be managed.

7. Wealth is a flow.

8. Wire transfers of deposits account for the bulk of monetary transactions.

9. The medium of exchange function becomes more important as the economy becomes more specialized.

10. If X can be bought or sold quickly and easily with no transaction costs, and the price does not change however long the buyer or seller searches for a better deal, then X is perfectly liquid.

Self-Test: Multiple Choice

1. Some believe commodity money is better than credit money because
   a. it is irrational to accept tokens in exchange for goods and services.
   b. the supply of credit money is often manipulated by governments to achieve short term goals.

c. the supply of commodity money never varies.
d. commodity money is more efficient in that it uses fewer resources.
e. All of the above.

2. Which of the following is not a medium of exchange?
   a. coin
   b. currency
   c. checkable deposits
   d. wire transfers
   e. passbook savings accounts

3. Money is a stock in the sense that
   a. it represents wealth just as stocks and bonds do.
   b. people like to stock up on money.
   c. a given quantity of it exists at any particular instant.
   d. money is defined only if a time interval is specified.
   e. All of the above.

4. Barter may replace money if
   a. inflation is rampant.
   b. prices are controlled.
   c. taxes are excessive.
   d. only credit money exists.
   e. All but d.

5. Which of the following is the most liquid?
   a. coin and currency
   b. bonds
   c. a house
   d. a passbook savings account
   e. stocks

6. Money and income
   a. are the same since more money is more income.
   b. are the same since we measure income in dollars.
   c. are different since money refers to the current holdings of media of exchange while income refers to the value of resources received in a given period of time.
   d. are different since money can be inherited but income is earned.
   e. are different since money is savings and income equals expenditures.

7. Monetary theory
   a. prescribes the tax and revenue strategies that governments ought to follow.
   b. describes the relationship between money, interest, income, and prices.

c. is concerned with how an individual bank ought to be run.

d. states that full-bodied commodity money is better than credit money.

e. prescribes a set of prudent practices that each of us ought to follow in managing our money.

8. Monetary policy

a. prescribes the tax and revenue policies that governments ought to follow.

b. is the formulation of prescriptive statements governing the creation and regulation of money.

c. makes use of monetary theory.

d. All of the above.

e. Only *b* and *c*.

Topics for Discussion

1. Describe the evolution from barter to indirect barter to the use of money.

2. Compare the transaction costs of storing wealth as money versus storing it as stocks and bonds.

3. Give an example where more than one monetary unit has been used to fulfill the three functions of money.

4. Describe how computer-based technology could change our conception of money.

5. In what sense is money a poor store of value?

Exercise Questions

1. Imagine an economy made up of the people and goods in Table 1.1 below. Each column refers to the good listed at the top and each row to the person listed at the left. A positive entry indicates the number of units of the good that someone has and is willing to sell. A negative entry indicates the number of units of the good that the person wants to buy. Each of these entries refers to either the quantities supplied or demanded given a price of one dollar for each good. For example, Gerry has two bushels of potatoes to sell. He wants to buy two hours of child guidance for his daughter.

   Notice that all the rows and columns add up to zero. That means we have an equilibrium price system. Each person is able to trade for what he wants and the quantities demanded and supplied are equal at the given prices.

Table 1.1   A Sample Economy

	Potatoes	Dance Lessons	Child Guidance
Gerry, the potato farmer	+2	0	–2
Jan, the dance instructor	–2	+2	0
Martin, the child psychologist	0	–2	+2

   a. Assume Gerry has two dollars. Construct a set of money-using
   trades that clears the market.

   b. Construct a set of barter or indirect barter transactions that
   clears the market. Remember that services such as dance lessons
   or child guidance cannot be passed through an intermediary.

2. The act of saving is very different in a monetary system than in a
   barter system. In a barter system, if Jan wants to save a potato,
   she simply sets it aside. In a monetary system, she would buy one
   less potato. So, at existing prices the quantity supplied of potatoes
   would be (*a:* greater than/equal to/less than) the quantity
   demanded. The price of potatoes would (*b:* rise/fall/not
   change). When she chooses to spend her money on potatoes in the
   next period, the price of potatoes would tend to (*c:* rise/fall).

   Therefore, under a barter system, Jan's decision to save (*d:* in-
   creases/decreases/does not affect) Gerry's income. Under a
   monetary system, Jan's decision to save (*e:* raises/lowers/does not
   affect) Gerry's current income but it (*f:* raises/lowers/does not
   affect) Gerry's future income.

   The simple Keynesian model predicts that consumption and
   current income will fall if savings increase. This makes sense in a
   (*g:* barter/monetary) system where the effects on future income
   are (*h:* considered/ignored). This illustrates the connection between
   money and recessions as well as the need for money in a complex,
   highly specialized, service-oriented society.

Answers to Self-Tests

Completion

1. commodity money
2. credit money
3. currency
4. indirect barter

5. standard of value
6. medium of exchange
7. near-money
8. *M-1*

True-False

1. False	6. False
2. True	7. False
3. False	8. True
4. False	9. True
5. True	10. True

Multiple Choice

1. *b*	5. *a*
2. *e*	6. *c*
3. *c*	7. *b*
4. *e*	8. *e*

Answers to Exercise Questions

1*a*. Gerry uses his two dollars to buy two hours of child psychology from Martin. Martin uses the same two dollars to buy two hours of dance instruction from Jan. Jan uses the same two dollars to buy two bushels of potatoes from Gerry.

b. Notice that no double coincidence of wants exists. Someone will have to accept a good in trade that they do not want in order to trade for what they do want. Next, since services like child psychology cannot be passed from one person to the next, this system does not have even an indirect barter solution unless Martin can be convinced to accept potatoes he does not want. Martin trades his service for two units of Gerry's potatoes. He then gives the potatoes to Jan in return for dance instruction. If Martin fails to see the opportunity, the others are powerless to act.

2*a*. greater than
 b. fall
 c. rise
 d. does not affect

e. lowers
f. raises
g. monetary
h. ignored

CHAPTER 2   The Financial System: An Overview

Learning Objectives

After studying this chapter, you should be able to

1. describe the intermediation function of financial intermediaries.

2. explain the four great advantages of financial intermediaries.

3. explain the three main types of risk.

4. explain how a low-risk portfolio can contain individual assets with large risks.

5. define hedging.

6. explain why the government regulates financial institutions.

7. explain why financial institutions have an incentive to take excessive risk from the depositor's point of view.

Key Terms, Concepts, and Institutions

You should be able to define or explain

financial intermediary
default risk
interest-rate (market) risk
portfolio
consumer ignorance

hedging
purchasing-power risk
diversification
risk-pooling

Self-Test: Completion

1. Risks for which payments to be received in the future will have less purchasing power due to unexpectedly high inflation are

   called _____ risks.

2. Financial intermediaries are institutions which buy claims from

   _____ and sell claims on themselves to _____.

3. _____ risk is the risk that a borrower will not be able to
   repay a loan.

4. Buying assets with offsetting risks is an example of portfolio

   _____.

5. Interest-rate (market) risk is the risk that the market value of a

   security will fall because interest rates _____.

6. One way to avoid financial risk is to _____, that is, to have
   one's assets and liabilities come due at the same time.

7. The closer to maturity a fixed-rate security is, the _____
   the interest-rate (market) risk. As the security nears maturity, the

   price of the security _____.

8. With respect to default risk, the safest assets are the obligations

   of the government and _____.

9. Usually, the higher the yield on a security, the _____ its risk.

10. The collection of assets one owns is called a _____.

Self-Test: True–False

1. If interest rates paid to depositors remain constant while other
   interest rates fall, the decisions by depositors of whether or not
   to withdraw deposits are not independent of each other.

2. Corporate bonds are more liquid than a deposit in a savings and
   loan association.

3. The closer to maturity a security is, the lower is the interest-rate
   risk.

4. A low-risk portfolio contains only assets that individually have
   small risk.

5. The intermediation function of financial intermediaries is to
   bring savers and borrowers together.

6. Suppose that current high yields on bonds are tempting to
   investors, but they fear that coming Treasury needs and the possibility of further problems with the money supply could push
   interest rates up in the near future. This type of risk is known as
   interest-rate risk.

7. With respect to default risk, corporate bonds are riskier than government bonds.

8. The government insures against losses all the assets offered by financial intermediaries.

9. When a financial intermediary receives funds from the public, it issues its own liabilities instead.

10. One rationale for government regulation of financial intermediaries is that consumers do not have the expertise to evaluate the soundness of the institutions.

Self-Test: Multiple Choice

1. The advantage(s) of using financial intermediaries is (are) that
   a. they can increase the maturity of the loan for the lender.
   b. they can minimize cost.
   c. they can pool risk.
   d. All of the above.
   e. b and c.

2. Which of the following exhibits the lowest degree of default risk?
   a. corporate bonds
   b. U.S. government bonds
   c. corporate stock
   d. commercial paper
   e. municipal bonds

3. According to the text, the best justification for regulating banks and other financial intermediaries is because
   a. consumers are ignorant.
   b. bank failures can result in a catastrophic reduction in the money supply.
   c. regulation is an effective way to reallocate resources.
   d. there are extensive economies of scale in banking.
   e. a and b.

4. Financial intermediaries can borrow short term to lend long term because
   a. long-term interest rates are higher than short-term interest rates.
   b. financial intermediaries generally have inside information about the stock market.
   c. if a group of depositors is large, their demand for cash is predictable.

d. information and transactions costs are smaller for financial intermediaries than they are for depositors.

e. government regulations encourage them to do so.

5. The fact that savings and loan associations borrow short and lend long leaves them exposed to
   a. default risk.
   b. purchasing-power risk.
   c. interest-rate risk.
   d. a liquidity crisis should a run on deposits develop.
   e. c and *d.*

6. Insured savings and time deposits offered by financial intermediaries have
   a. no default risk.
   b. no purchasing-power risk.
   c. high interest-rate risk.
   d. All of the above.
   e. Only *a* and *c.*

7. Financial intermediaries
   a. extend short-term loans even though their sources of funds are primarily long term in nature.
   b. extend long-term loans even though their sources of funds are primarily short term in nature.
   c. tie their loans to specific deposit liabilities.
   d. are always protected from unexpected deposit outflows by the law of large numbers.
   e. All of the above.

8. Unexpectedly high inflation
   a. increases purchasing-power risk for the borrower.
   b. decreases purchasing-power risk for the borrower.
   c. increases purchasing-power risk for the lender.
   d. decreases purchasing-power risk for the lender.
   e. b and *c.*

9. Interest-rate risk can be reduced by
   a. lending only long term.
   b. government insurance on deposits.
   c. hedging.
   d. borrowing at fixed rates of interest.
   e. lending at a fixed rate of interest.

10. The closer to maturity a fixed rate bond is
    a. the greater the risk of default.
    b. the greater the purchasing-power risk.

c. the higher the interest-rate risk.

d. the lower the risk of default.

e. the lower the interest-rate risk.

Topics for Discussion

1. A broker performs a pure search function by bringing potential borrowers and lenders together and receives a fee or commission for this service. Unlike a dealer, a broker does not take legal possession of the claims traded. Are the broker's services an inter-mediation activity as defined by the text? Be prepared to defend your answer.

2. Explain why financial intermediaries can reduce costs.

3. Give an example of a circumstance where the decisions of depositors will not be independent of each other, so that banks will not be able to predict deposit outflows accurately.

4. Suppose that you anticipate that the rate of inflation will in-crease to 10 percent this year. Would you rather be a lender hold-ing on to a $5,000 bond which pays a fixed 8 percent interest, or the borrower who issued the bond? Be prepared to defend your answer.

5. Consider the following assets:

   insured savings and time deposits
   short-term government securities
   long-term government securities
   corporate bonds
   corporate stock

   Which assets are safest in terms of default risk? Why? What happens to the yield as the risk of default increases?

Exercise Questions

1. Assume a market for a one-year security in which borrowers and lenders deal directly with each other. The observed rate at which the security is traded is 12 percent.

   a. Since both the borrower and the lender incur costs in seeking each other out, the 12 percent rate (is/is not) the effective cost to the borrower, (and/nor) the effective return to the lender.

   b. A premium is the compensation that an economic unit receives to induce it to bear a particular type of risk. Assume equal

-11-

information and transaction costs to both the borrower and the lender of 4 percent. Since the lender is taking the risk that the borrower will not be able to repay the loan, assume a

_____ premium of 2 percent to compensate the lender for the risk of default. Since the lender's funds will be tied up for a year, assume a liquidity premium of 1 percent is necessary to compensate the lender for this loss of liquidity. The effective return to the lender (the actual return plus any implicit benefits and minus any implicit costs) is the observed rate (plus/minus) information and transactions costs, the default premium, and the liquidity premium. The effective cost to the borrower is the observed rate (plus/minus) information and transactions costs.

Without intermediation, the effective rate of return to the

lender is _____ percent, and the effective cost to the

borrower is _____ percent.

2. A financial intermediary is set up to collect the funds of savers and make loans to borrowers, so we would expect information and transactions costs to be (*a:* greater/less) for the financial intermediary than for individual borrowers and savers.

   b. Assume the information and transactions costs are 1 percent for the Uriskit National Bank. Uriskit also has a lower default premium, about 1 percent, due to its expertise in credit evaluation and its ability to pool risk. Uriskit's funds will be tied up for one year in this security, so assume a liquidity premium of 1 percent. Because Uriskit is a profit-motivated institution, it charges a fee of 1 percent for its services. Then the rate that Uriskit could pay to lenders (depositors) is the going rate of 12 percent (plus/minus) information costs and transactions costs, the default and liquidity premiums, and its fee, or

   _____ percent.

   c. This rate (is/is not) the effective rate of return to the lender, because the lender still incurs information and transaction costs even if a financial intermediary is used. However, these costs are usually substantially (more/less) than if they had dealt directly with the borrower. Likewise, the lender still has some default risk and loses some liquidity, but again these premiums will be less than if the lender had dealt directly with the borrower. Assume that, by going through the financial intermediary, information and transactions costs are reduced to 1 percent for both the borrower and the lender, and the default and liquidity premiums to the lender are reduced to ½ percent each.

If the borrower and the lender go through a financial intermediary, the effective return to the lender is _____ percent.

If the borrower and the lender go through a financial intermediary, the net cost to the borrower is the observed rate

(plus/minus) information and transaction costs, or _____ percent.

Using the financial intermediary (increased/decreased) the effective return to the lender and (increased/decreased) the effective cost to the borrower.

3. The following exercise is designed to illustrate the advantages of diversification and risk pooling.

Suppose that you have $10,000 to invest and have three options:
Option *a:* You can buy a U.S. government security which offers a guaranteed return of 8 percent.
Option *b:* You can buy one of three private loans, offering a 15 percent rate of return. One of these will default, but you don't know which one. Each loan therefore has a $2/3$ chance of a 15 percent return, and a $1/3$ chance of a 0 percent return.
Option *c:* You can pool your money with three other investors, buy all four assets, and split the earnings.

What is your expected dollar amount of return for each option?

Option *a:* $

Option *b:* $

. Option *c:* $

Discuss the relevant risk and return of each option.

4. If the market interest rate on a bond is i, the present value (PV) of the payment (A) to be received at maturity, which is t years in the future, is given by the formula

$$PV = \frac{A}{(1 + i)^t}.$$

An investor would be willing to pay the present value (or less) to buy the bond today.

a. Suppose that you buy a five-year bond which has a maturity value of $5,000 and the market interest rate is 8 percent. What is the highest price that you would be willing to pay for this bond?

b. Suppose that the day after you buy the bond, the market interest rate rises to 10 percent. If you had to sell the bond in a hurry to raise cash, what is the highest price you can expect to receive?

As the market interest rate rises, the prices of bonds (rise/fall).

c. Suppose you keep the bond for three years, and then sell it. If the market interest rate stayed at 8 percent, what is the highest price you can expect to receive for this bond with two years remaining to maturity?

As the length of time to maturity decreases, the prices of bonds (increase/decrease).

Answers to Self-Tests

Completion

1. purchasing-power
2. borrowers; lenders (savers)
3. Default
4. diversification
5. rise

6. hedge
7. lower; approaches its face value
8. financial intermediaries
9. greater
10. portfolio

True–False

1. True (*Everyone* will want to increase their deposits.)
2. False
3. True
4. False
5. False (They buy securities from borrowers and issue claims on themselves.)
6. True
7. True
8. False
9. True
10. True

Multiple Choice

1. *e*
2. *b*
3. *e*
4. *c*
5. *e*

6. *a*
7. *b*
8. *e*
9. *c*
10. *e*

Answers to Exercise Questions

1a. is not; nor

 b. default; minus; plus; 5 percent; 16 percent

2a. less

 b. minus; 8 percent

 c. is not; less; 6 percent; plus; 13 percent; increased; decreased

3. Option *a:* 8 percent of $10,000 = $800.

 Option *b:* You have a $\frac{2}{3}$ chance of receiving 15 percent of $10,000, or $1,500, and a $\frac{1}{3}$ chance of receiving nothing. Your expected rate of return is $\frac{2}{3}$ ($1,500) + $\frac{1}{3}$ (0) = $1,000.

 Option *c:* Your group buys the government bond and gets $800 and the three bonds, one of which goes sour. Your group gets 15 percent of $10,000 from each of the two good bonds, and nothing from the one which fails. You get $800 + $3,000 = $3,800 altogether, or $950 each. Each of you accepted a small certain loss to protect yourself against the possibility of a greater loss.

4a. $5,000/(1 + .08)^5 = $3,402.92.

 b. $5,000/(1 + .10)^5 = $3,104.61; fall.

 c. $5,000/(1 + .08)^2 = $4,286.69; increase.

CHAPTER 3   The Banking Industry

Learning Objectives

After studying this chapter, you should be able to

1. understand the evolution from state banking to national banking to the Federal Reserve System.

2. understand the functions of bank regulations that limit competition.

3. explain the rules governing branch banking, interstate banking, bank holding companies, and capital asset ratios.

4. describe the impact of rules governing branch banking, interstate banking, and capital asset ratios.

5. appreciate the roles the FDIC, the Fed, and the Comptroller of the Currency currently play in regulating and serving the banking industry.

Key Terms, Concepts, and Institutions

You should be able to define or explain

bank notes
state bank
central bank
national bank
charter
Comptroller of the Currency
Federal Reserve System
FDIC
stockholders' equity
capital/asset ratio
forced merger

correspondent banking
city correspondent
country correspondent
bank holding company
bank concentration
economies of scale
interstate banking
branch banking
unit banking
redlining

Self-Test: Completion

1. If a state allows only one office for any bank then it is a _____ state.

2. If larger banks earned a higher rate of return than smaller banks this would be evidence of _____ in banking.

3. The period of state banking ended in 1863 with the creation of _____.

4. Under a law passed in _____ the Fed must charge for the services it provides.

5. The practice of refusing to lend within a geographical area, perhaps an inner city, is called _____. The practice is prohibited under the _____ Act.

6. The FDIC, while it can close a failing bank, is more likely to _____ the bank.

7. Under the Federal Reserve System, reserves are held either in the bank's own vault as cash or at the _____.

8. The reserve requirements for all institutions with checkable deposits will be the same by _____.

9. A small bank that maintains deposits at a large bank in return for advice, access to national money markets, and loan participation arrangements is called a _____.

10. Laws that set ceilings on interest rates on loans are called _____ laws.

11. Banks within a single city use a _____ to net out checks written against each other.

12. In banking, *capital* refers to _____.

Self-Test: True-False

1. A bank with a 100 percent capital/asset ratio could not make loans.

2. Banks are chartered in order to increase competition.

3. The FDIC has proposed that higher risk banks ought to pay higher premiums.

-17-

4. Bank holding company acquisitions are regulated by the Fed.

5. Nationally, the top five banks control more than half the deposits.

6. Unit banking reduces statewide concentration ratios.

7. The distinction between being a member of the Fed or not is fading.

8. The FDIC generally closes failed banks.

9. There are no exceptions to the prohibition of multi-state deposit collection.

10. Correspondence banking allows banks to participate in loans made in other states.

Self-Test: Multiple Choice

1. One of the problems with the national banking system was
   a. inadequate check clearing.
   b. rapid fluctuations in the money supply.
   c. charters issued capriciously by the state legislatures.
   d. lack of a uniform bank note.
   e. during a crisis reserves flowed from country to city banks.

2. The Federal Reserve System
   a. allowed banks to maintain reserves at big city banks.
   b. monopolizes the check-clearing business.
   c. allows institutions with reserves at the Fed to borrow from the Fed.
   d. consists of all state and national banks.
   e. has been able to prevent depressions and massive bank failures.

3. To some degree we already have interstate banking because of all of the following *except:*
   a. Bank holding companies can buy anything they can afford.
   b. Banks can make loans nationwide; only deposit collection is restricted to one state.
   c. Regulators have allowed some interstate mergers.
   d. Correspondence networks can be nationwide.
   e. Some bank holding companies made interstate banking acquisitions before they were illegal.

4. The $100,000 ceiling on deposit insurance exists because
   a. even this limited level of insurance significantly reduces bank profits.
   b. people with more money are smarter and will not need the insurance.

c. private insurance is widespread for the larger deposits.

d. it was established when few deposits were over $100,000 and has not been changed.

e. the FDIC hopes the larger depositors will monitor the bank's safety and pressure banks to be safe.

5. Bank charters are granted only if the bank would not take too much business away from existing banks because

    a. the Comptroller of the Currency is solely concerned with the profit of bankers.

    b. excessive competition reduces innovation in banking.

    c. the increased spending by new banks on buildings and equipment would raise costs to customers.

    d. less competition would mean fewer failures and bank failures affect the general public, not just stockholders.

    e. regulators would rather have fewer banks to regulate.

6. Regulators can only urge or attempt to convince a bank that more capital is required except when

    a. the bank is small.

    b. the bank is asking for a privilege.

    c. the bank is owned by a bank holding company.

    d. the bank has a state charter.

    e. the bank does not have FDIC insurance.

7. A higher capital/asset ratio increases bank safety because

    a. with more capital a bank run is less likely to exhaust reserves.

    b. the bigger the stockholders' share, the larger percentage loss a bank can sustain before depositors' funds are jeopardized.

    c. more capital allows a bank flexibility in pursuing profit opportunities as they arise.

    d. more capital means the bank has more buildings and equipment which could be sold in desperate times.

    e. All but d.

8. Banks are likely to choose a capital/asset ratio that is too low from a social point of view because they are _____ interested in their own rate of return and _____ interested in safety than the public.

    a. more, more

    b. more, less

    c. less, more

    d. less, less

    e. equally, less

9. Since the creation of the FDIC in 1934

    a. the frequency of bank failures has declined steadily.

b. runs on banks by insured depositors have been rare.

c. when banks fail, depositors over the insured limit have been routinely wiped out.

d. the FDIC has come to manage a large number of banks.

e. the premiums have proven insufficient to cover losses.

10. Continental Illinois
    a. deposits over $100,000 suffered an 80 percent loss.
    b. deposits were mostly small passbook accounts.
    c. was, as with most problem banks, merged with another bank.
    d. managers were praised for their good work and kept on the job.
    e. is a rare example of the FDIC taking control of a failing institution.

Topics for Discussion

1. Why might unit banking reduce competition in rural areas?

2. How did the Federal Reserve Act of 1913 provide for a flexible currency?

3. Why were the charters of the first two central banks of the U.S. allowed to expire?

4. How was free banking beneficial?

5. Describe some limitations to the powers of regulators and examiners.

6. Describe how bank competition and failure can be beneficial.

7. Why doesn't the FDIC insure all depositors?

8. Why do we insure depositors at all? Why can't we rely on depositors to discipline unsafe banks by withdrawing their funds?

9. Argue for or against the proposal that banks should be able to buy a lower capital/asset ratio by paying a higher insurance rate.

10. Argue for or against interstate banking.

Exercise Questions

1. Currently, the Bank of Growth has assets totaling $.5 billion and stockholders' equity of $30 million. The capital/asset ratio is

    (a: _____) percent. Since $30 million in assets was raised from stockholders, the other $470 million must represent the depositors' contributions. The rate paid depositors averages 7 percent and the earnings from assets average 8 percent. So the bank earns (*b:* _____) million from their assets in a given year. In the same year they owe depositors (*c:* _____) million which leaves them earnings before operating expenses of (*d:* _____) million. If operating expenses are $2 million then (*e:* _____) million is left to distribute to stockholders who receive a (*f:* _____) percent return.

2. The Bank of Safety also has $.5 billion of assets and operating expenses of $2 million. If $50 million represents stockholders' equity, then the capital/asset ratio is (*a:* _____) percent. The Bank of Safety also earns 8 percent on assets so they earn (*b:* _____) million just as the Bank of Growth does. There are (*c:* _____) million of deposits earning an average of 7 percent so depositors are owed (*d:* _____) in the current year. After the operating expenses, this leaves (*e:* _____) million to distribute to stockholders who receive a (*f:* _____) percent return.

3. Consider what would happen to these two banks if next year interest rates rose. Depositors would have the option of withdrawing their money and investing it elsewhere. Banks sign loan contracts that typically last a couple of years or more. Therefore, while the banks may be locked into earning 8 percent, depositors could demand 9 percent.

   The Bank of Growth still earns (*a:* _____) million but now owes depositors (*b:* _____) million. After operating expenses of $2 million there is a deficit of (*c:* _____) million that must be taken from stockholders. The stockholders' rate of return is a negative (*d:* _____) percent.

4. The Bank of Safety faces the same situation. Depositors earn 9 percent, assets 8 percent. Earnings total (*a:* _____) million as before. Depositors must be paid (*b:* _____) million. After operating expenses of $2 million a deficit of (*c:* _____) remains which must be taken from stockholders' equity. The return to stockholders is a negative (*d:* _____) percent.

5. On June 16, 1983, the *Wall Street Journal* provided an illustration of the problems of insufficient capital. Imperial Bank of California, which had been one of the industry's fastest growing and most profitable banks, was having some problems. Imperial Bank's growth was due in part to a relatively low ratio of shareholders' equity to total deposits of 4.9 percent. The turnabout came quickly as builders defaulted on construction loans. Imperial had 30 percent of its assets in construction loans. As a result, Imperial Bank was involved in discussions with the California Superintendent of Banks, the Federal Reserve Bank of San Francisco, and the FDIC. These discussions led Imperial Bank to sign an agreement to raise its capital/asset ratio to 7.2 percent by January 1984. How is this example related to the exercise? How will the higher capital/asset ratio rein in the runaway Imperial Bank?

Answers to Self-Tests

Completion

1. unit banking
2. economies of scale
3. the National Banking System
4. 1980
5. redlining, Community Reinvestment
6. merge
7. Fed
8. 1988
9. country correspondent
10. usury
11. clearinghouse
12. stockholders' equity

True–False

1. False	6. True
2. False	7. True
3. True	8. False
4. True	9. False
5. False	10. True

Answers to Exercise Questions

1*a*. 6   3*a*. $40
 b. $40   *b*. $42.3
 c. $32.9   *c*. $4.3
 d. $7.1   *d*. 14$^{1}/_{3}$
 e. $5.1
 f. 17   4*a*. $40
                            b. $40.5
2*a*. 10   *c*. $2.5
 b. $40   *d*. 5
 c. $450
 d. $31.5
 e. 6.5
 f. 13

5. Imperial Bank is like the Bank of Growth. As long as its earnings were greater than the payments to depositors the profits could be distributed to a small ownership base. However, losses—in this case default losses—also are drawn from the small ownership base. With the higher capital/asset requirement, Imperial will either have to scale down deposits and assets or broaden its ownership base.

CHAPTER 4   The Banking Firm

Learning Objectives

After studying this chapter, you should be able to

1. describe the bank's balance sheet, define each item and determine whether it is an asset or a liability.

2. show which assets are considered primary or secondary reserves.

3. understand how compensating balances raise the effective interest rate for a borrower.

4. distinguish between asset management and liability management.

5. explain the risk a bank takes if the maturities of its assets and liabilities are seriously mismatched.

6. explain the different types of business loans.

7. list other services that banks perform, besides taking deposits and making loans.

Key Terms, Concepts, and Institutions

You should be able to define or explain

standby letter of credit
checkable deposits
demand deposits
money-market account
NOW account
Super-NOW account
implicit interest
collateral
revolving credit
service balances
note-issuing facility

secondary reserves
commercial paper
call loans
credit rationing
customer relationship
term loans
line of credit
compensating (or supporting)
  balances
prime rate
trade acceptance

time deposits
passbook savings account
nonnegotiable certificate of
   deposit
negotiable certificate of deposit
amortize
federal funds
banker's acceptance
earning assets
primary reserves

cash items in the process of
   collection
transactions accounts
reserve requirement as a tax
asset management
liability management
repurchase agreements
Eurodollar
LIBOR
mortgage loan

Self-Test: Completion

1. A large proportion of banks' liabilities are _____ term, while most of their assets are _____ term.

2. Convenient branches and provision of free services are ways that banks pay _____ interest on demand deposits.

3. The actual maturity of mortgage loans is (greater/less) than their stated maturity.

4. Most consumer loans are made for the purchase of _____.

5. Usually, long-term interest rates are (higher/lower) than short-term rates.

6. If banks expect interest rates to rise, they should buy (long-/short-) term securities.

7. If a seller draws an order to pay on a buyer's bank, and the order is accepted, it is known as a _____.

8. The larger the loan, the (higher/lower) the interest rate, all other things being equal.

9. _____ are loans made to security dealers and brokers, often on a (renewable) one-day basis.

10. If a bank sold Treasury bills to acquire funds, this action would be characterized as (asset/liability) management.

Self-Test: True–False

1. The federal-funds rate is the rate the Fed charges eligible institutions to borrow from it.

2. A line of credit is an arrangement whereby the bank agrees to make loans up to a certain amount almost on demand.

3. Anyone can buy a negotiable certificate of deposit.

4. The purpose of reserve requirements is to ensure the safety of the depositors' funds.

5. Selling Treasury bills to increase liquidity is an example of liability management.

6. A compensating balance requirement is legally binding on the borrower.

7. A bank needing liquidity might buy federal funds.

8. Cash items in the process of collection are extremely liquid and count as a part of primary reserves.

9. Compensating balances reduce the effective interest cost to the borrower.

10. The prime rate is the highest rate a bank would charge a borrower.

Self-Test: Multiple Choice

1. A bank's primary reserves consist of
   a. demand deposits with other banks.
   b. vault cash.
   c. reserves with the Fed.
   d. All of the above.
   e. Only b and c.

2. Which of the following would a bank hold as part of secondary reserves?
   a. vault cash
   b. Treasury bills
   c. CIPC
   d. deposits at the Fed
   e. demand deposits

3. If the Treasury-bill rate is less than the federal-funds rate but greater than the rate on negotiable certificates of deposits, then a bank needing funds would be likely to
   a. sell Treasury bills.
   b. borrow federal funds.
   c. buy federal funds.
   d. buy negotiable certificates of deposit.
   e. issue negotiable certificates of deposit.

4. Small banks are likely to use which of the following instruments of liability management?
   a. repurchase agreements
   b. negotiable CDs
   c. Eurodollars
   d. federal funds
   e. commercial paper.

5. Which of the following are *not* liquid assets for a bank?
   a. consumer loans
   b. call loans
   c. mortgage loans
   d. All of the above are liquid loans.
   e. Only *a* and *b.*

6. Banks perform other services besides taking deposits and making loans. Which of the following activities are banks *not* permitted to undertake?
   a. payroll preparation
   b. acting as dealers in the money markets
   c. acting as brokers in the real estate market
   d. administering trusts
   e. acting as dealers in the foreign exchange market

7. There have been proposals to take trust departments away from banks and turn them into separate institutions. An argument in favor of separating banking and trust activities is that
   a. banks might not separate their trust and commercial banking activities.
   b. banks are not permitted to buy equity securities for trust accounts.
   c. banks lack the expertise for investment or financial advising.
   d. trusts allow banks to accumulate great economic power.
   e. *a* and *d.*

8. Which of the following types of loans are *not* guaranteed or subsidized by the federal government?
   a. FHA mortgages
   b. student loans
   c. VA mortgages
   d. loans to foreign governments
   e. All of the above are guaranteed or subsidized by the federal government.

9. The higher the interest rate charged on loans is,
    a. the smaller the loan is.
    b. the greater the term of the loan.
    c. the more risky the loan is.
    d. the greater the demand for credit.
    e. All of the above are correct.

10. If portfolio managers appear to be shortening the maturities of their holdings of international bonds denominated in U.S. dollars, they probably anticipate
    a. U.S. interest rates to rise.
    b. U.S. interest rates to fall.
    c. U.S. bond prices to rise.
    d. b and c.
    e. a and c.

Topics for Discussion

1. What prevents a foreign government from declaring its debts null and void?

2. Which assets count as legal reserves for members of the Federal Reserve System?

3. Why do banks have an incentive to reschedule the loan payments of debtor countries who otherwise would default?

4. Suppose you are a real estate developer. Your income is variable, but you have a fixed monthly payroll. Would you prefer to have a term loan or a line of credit? Explain your answer.

5. Would a Treasury bond appear on a bank's books as a loan or a security purchase? How do loans differ from security purchases?

Exercise Questions

1. For each of the balance-sheet items in Table 4.1, indicate whether the item is an asset or a liability. If the item is an asset, indicate whether the item may be considered part of primary reserves, secondary reserves, or earning assets.

Table 4.1 Balance-Sheet Exercise

| | Asset | | | |
Item	Primary Reserves	Secondary Reserves	Earning Assets	Liability
Federal funds purchased				
Short-term U.S. government securities				
Money-market accounts				
Federal funds sold				
Banker's acceptances				
NOW accounts				
Vault cash				
Reserves at the Fed				
Call loans				
Term loans				
Passbook savings accounts				
Real estate loans				
Demand deposits				

2. Suppose the First National Bank of Greentree makes a $150,000 loan to the Mark FitzGerald Landscaping Service at a 12 percent interest rate with a 15 percent minimum compensating balance.

   a. How much of the $150,000 is actually available for Mark FitzGerald to use? $_____.

   b. What is the effective rate of interest on this amount?

   _____ percent.

   c. Mr. FitzGerald feels that 12 percent interest is awfully high for his loan. What might he do to get First National to offer him a lower rate?

   d. Suppose Mr. FitzGerald violates his minimum compensating balances requirement. What can the bank do?

Crossword Puzzle

2. _____ is considered to be part of a bank's primary reserves.
4. This type of loan is often rescheduled if the borrower cannot pay.
5. Business loans with a maturity of one to five years.

9. Supporting or _____ balances.

11. _____ bills.
12. Deposits traded among banks and other institutions.
13. Involve personal relationships with borrowers.
14. The rate banks charge their best customers.

15. Banks may not pay interest on _____ deposits.

16. _____ reserves include short-term government securities, banker's acceptances, and commercial paper.
17. Dollar-denominated deposits in European and Caribbean banks.
18. The rate at which large international banks lend to each other on the international market (abbreviation).

1. An arrangement whereby the bank agrees to make loans to a firm up to a certain amount almost on demand.

3. _____ market account.
5. Another type of bank activity.
6. A way to pay implicit interest on demand deposits (abbreviation).
7. The most familiar type of savings account.

8. Banker's _____.
9. Certificates of deposit (abbreviation).
10. Loans to dealers and brokers.
19. Checks that have just been deposited but have not been cleared (abbreviation).

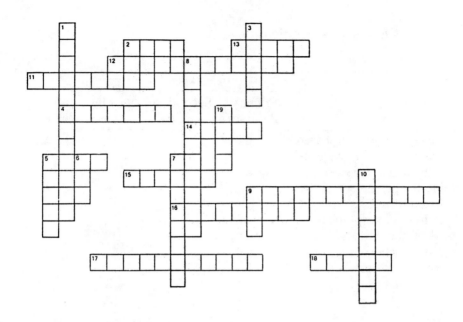

Answers to Self-Tests

Completion

1. short; long
2. implicit
3. less
4. durables
5. higher

6. short
7. banker's acceptance
8. lower
9. call loans
10. asset

True–False

1. False
2. True
3. True (If they have the money.)
4. False
5. False

6. False
7. True
8. False
9. False
10. False

Multiple Choice

1. *d*
2. *b*
3. *e*
4. *d*
5. *c*

6. *c*
7. *e*
8. *e*
9. *e*
10. *a*

Answers to Exercise Questions

1.

Item	Asset — Primary Reserves	Asset — Secondary Reserves	Asset — Earning Assets	Liability
Federal funds purchased	X			X
Short-term U.S. government securities		X	X	
Money-market accounts				X
Federal funds sold			X	
Banker's acceptances				X
NOW accounts				X
Vault cash	X			
Reserves at the Fed	X			
Call loans		X	X	
Term loans			X	
Passbook savings accounts				X
Real estate loans			X	
Demand deposits				X

2a. $127,500

 b. 14.12 percent. Mr. FitzGerald must pay 12 percent of $150,000, or $18,000 in interest. Since he can only use $127,500, the effective rate of interest is $18,000/$127,500 = 14.12 percent.

 c. He could offer to provide collateral, making the loan less risky for the bank.

 d. Nothing, legally, but the bank may refuse him further loans, or charge him a higher interest rate on future loans.

Answer to Crossword Puzzle

CHAPTER 5   Other Financial Intermediaries

Learning Objectives

After studying this chapter you should be able to

1. contrast the asset and liability composition of the major non-bank financial intermediaries and understand why they are composed differently.

2. describe the evolution of thrift institutions.

3. appreciate the seesawing, competitive struggle between banks, savings and loans, and securities.

4. explain the process of disintermediation and unusually high failure rates of savings and loan associations from the 1970s to mid-1980s.

5. explain how Regulation Q channeled funds from middle and lower income depositors to banks and thrifts.

6. explain how Regulation Q encouraged the creation of money-market funds and encouraged banks and thrifts to offer more and more services.

Key Terms, Concepts, and Institutions

You should be able to define or explain

thrift institutions	Federal National Mortgage
savings banks	Association
savings and loans	farm credit agencies
money-market funds	loading
credit unions	mutual fund
Regulation Q	maturity matching
disintermediation	ordinary life insurance

insurance
pension funds
Federal Home Loan Bank

term insurance
price discrimination

Self-Test: Completion

1. Consumer loans account for most of the assets of _____.

2. Many common-stock mutual funds charge a fee to cover brokerage commissions and other selling expenses. This fee is called a _____ charge.

3. Funds that give investors the opportunity to buy shares in a managed group of investments are called _____ funds.

4. The demise of the state insurance systems demonstrates that to be fully effective deposit insurance has to be backed by _____.

5. Variable-rate loans helped reduce the _____ gap at thrifts.

6. The agency that sells its own securities and makes the proceeds available to savings and loan associations is the _____.

7. _____ are financial intermediaries with both long-term assets and long-term liabilities.

8. The flow of funds from regulated intermediaries to the money markets during periods of high interest rates is called _____.

9. The form of insurance that does not build up an asset is known as _____ insurance.

10. If an institution allocates credit to preferred customers rather than raise loan rates then they are said to _____ credit.

Self-Test: True–False

1. Urbanization has reduced the need for life insurance as people have grown more self-sufficient and secure.

2. Savings and loan associations experienced their most rapid period of growth in 1981.

3. The earnings of mutual savings banks in excess of operating costs are either paid out to depositors or retained as a loan loss reserve.

4. The Federal Home Loan Banks supervise all savings and loan associations.

5. Savings and loans may not all offer precisely the same service at precisely the same price in part because location and convenience factors help differentiate the thrifts' products.

6. Thrifts have a comparative advantage in home loans because they know their local market better than a national insurance firm can.

7. Life insurance companies are the only group of institutions whose portfolio choices offer a direct link between the yields on municipal bonds and anticipated yields on common stock.

8. An increase in interest rates can make savings and loan associations unprofitable.

9. Thrifts were encouraged to lengthen the maturities of their liabilities to reduce their exposure to interest-rate risk.

10. It has been argued that the interest-rate ceilings discriminated against less wealthy households.

11. It is a basic principle of economics that if you block one channel of competition, you inadvertently block others.

12. Disintermediation refers to people pulling funds out of Regulation Q-restricted intermediaries to invest themselves.

Self-Test: Multiple Choice

1. The "let's pretend" policy of the FSLIC included
   a. allowing merged institutions to show a larger net worth than the sum of the two independent institutions' net worth.
   b. forcing savings and loans to record their loans at market value rather than historical value.
   c. allowing thrifts that, by all past definitions, had failed to remain open.
   d. estimating the thrift's income by assuming all loans paid current market rates.
   e. a and c.

2. Which of the following financial intermediaries tend to be organized on a mutual basis?
   a. savings and loan associations
   b. commercial banks
   c. life insurance companies

d. None of the above.

e. All of the above.

3. Which of the following intermediaries has the shortest term assets?

   a. money-market funds

   b. commercial banks

   c. life insurance companies

   d. savings and loan associations

   e. mutual savings banks

4. Which organization is found in the fewest states?

   a. commercial banks

   b. life insurance companies

   c. savings and loan associations

   d. mutual savings banks

   e. credit unions

5. While for a time the failure of savings and loans could be blamed on suddenly higher interest rates, lower rates have not ended the failures because

   a. fraud at thrifts has reached epidemic proportions.

   b. the housing market has failed to rebound despite lower interest rates.

   c. loan losses at thrifts have been higher, perhaps due to thrifts embarking on new, unfamiliar businesses.

   d. the failure of some state thrift insurance systems has called the national insurance system into question and depositors demand a higher interest rate to bear the added risk.

   e. the past failures have increased the cost of insurance which is now high enough to be causing some failures.

6. Which of the following is not a financial intermediary?

   a. commercial banks

   b. savings and loan associations

   c. Federal National Mortgage Association

   d. life insurance companies

   e. All the above are financial intermediaries.

7. Due to the term characteristics of their assets and liabilities, thrift institutions tend to experience problems when

   a. long-term interest rates rise.

   b. financial intermediation occurs.

   c. the effects of falling interest rates cause withdrawals of deposits from thrifts.

   d. short-term interest rates rise sharply.

   e. None of the above.

8. The types of assets purchased by financial intermediaries are determined by
   a. legal restrictions.
   b. tax considerations.
   c. riskiness.
   d. the term structure of their liabilities.
   e. available yield.
   f. All of the above.
   g. Only a and d.

9. Regulation Q is often criticized because it
   a. distorts resource allocation.
   b. discriminates against small savers.
   c. protects thrift institutions.
   d. All of the above.
   e. None of the above.

10. Regulation Q was supposed to help thrifts by
   a. reducing the interest rate thrifts would have to pay to attract funds.
   b. reducing the flow of funds to thrifts.
   c. giving thrifts the right to offer variable interest-rate mortgages.
   d. providing thrifts with a secondary mortgage market.
   e. allowing thrifts to enter other businesses.

Topics for Discussion

1. How did depository institutions compete with each other for deposits after Regulation Q ceilings suppressed explicit interest-rate competition?

2. An individual thrift institution competes with other thrifts and commercial banks for savings deposits. What other source of competition for thrifts is not subject to Regulation Q ceilings?

3. Why did commercial banks and thrift institutions begin offering short-term certificates of deposit?

4. Anyone can follow his or her own saving and investment plan while working and then retire on the income from the plan, or buy an annuity. Alternatively, one can save for retirement through a pension plan at work. What is the advantage of saving through a pension fund?

5. Why do life insurance companies prefer to buy corporate bonds, while marine, fire, and casualty insurance companies prefer municipal bonds?

Exercise Questions

The purpose of this exercise is to bring home the magnitude and causes of the crisis in savings and loans. You will be given some data and you will use the material in the chapter to interpret the data. All dollar figures are in billions.[1]

	Number of Thrifts with Negative Net Worth		Assets of Thrifts with Net Worth < 0		Assets of Failed
Year	GAAP[a]	RAP	GAAP	RAP	Institutions
1980	17	17	$.127	$.127	$2.9
1981	65	41	$17.3	$7.1	$15.1
1982	201	80	$48.7	$13.1	$46.8
1983	287	54	$78.9	$12.6	$15.9
1984	434	71	$107.3	$12.0	$9.5

[a]GAAP refers to generally accepted accounting principles. RAP refers to regulatory accounting principles.

1. Why are GAAP and RAP different?

2. When did the differences appear?

3. Have the differences been narrowing or widening?

4. Assets of failed institutions refers to the assets of the institutions the FSLIC actually closed or merged. Compare these assets with the assets of thrifts with a GAAP net worth less than 0. How has the policy of FSLIC closings changed?

5. How might this policy change affect the behavior of thrifts?

---

[1] All data (except new mortgage rates) are taken from "Insolvency and Risk Taking in the Thrift Industry: Implications for the Future" by James R. Barth, R. Dan Brumbaugh, Daniel Sauerhaft, and George H. K. Wang, *Contemporary Policy Issues*, Vol. 3, No. 5, pp. 1–32. See Tables 2, 3, 5, and 9. The new mortgage rates are from the Federal Reserve Bulletin, various issues.

Year	FSLIC Reserves	Cost of Solution[a]	Cost of Assistance Undertaken	New Mortgage Rates	Market Value (Net Worth/ Assets)
1980	$6.5	$.01	$.166	12.65	−12.47
1981	$6.3	$1.23	$.988	14.74	−17.32
1982	$6.3	$1.95	$1.127	15.12	−12.03
1983	$6.4	$4.18	$.934	12.66	−5.64
1984	$5.9	$15.77	$.849	12.37	−2.74

[a]The cost of solution refers to the present value cost of the least expensive solution (usually merging) for institutions with a negative GAAP net worth. The cost of assistance undertaken is the present value costs of the new assistance cases undertaken that year. The new mortgage rate is the average effective rate on conventional mortgages on new homes assuming prepayment at the end of 10 years. The market value of net worth/assets is net worth calculated by market value divided by thrift industry assets.

6. Why did thrift failures increase just as the rate they earned on new loans increased in 1981 and 1982?

7. Despite the drop in interest rates in 1983 and 1984 more thrifts' GAAP net worth became negative. Why?

8. Could the FSLIC have afforded to close all the thrifts with a negative GAAP net worth in 1984?

9. Why did the market value of the industry improve so much in 1983 and 1984?

10. How is it possible for more institutions to have a negative GAAP net worth at the same time the market value net worth of the industry as a whole is improving?

11. Match these principal assets and principal liabilities with each type of financial intermediary listed below. A financial intermediary may have more than one principal asset or liability.

Principal Assets

A. corporate stock
B. mortgages
C. U.S. government securities
D. business loans
E. municipal bonds
F. corporate bonds
G. commercial paper
H. bank certificates of deposit
I. cash
J. consumer loans

Principal Liabilities

1. insurance policies
2. demand deposits
3. pension-fund reserves
4. time deposits
5. shares
6. government agency bonds

Type of Intermediary	Principal Asset(s)	Principal Liability(ies)
Commercial banks		
Savings and loans		
Mutual savings banks		
Money-market funds		
Mutual funds		
Life insurance companies		
Pension funds		
Marine, fire, and casualty insurance companies		
Government agencies		
Credit unions		

Answers to Self-Tests

Completion

1. credit unions
2. loading
3. mutual
4. the national government
5. maturity
6. Federal National Mortgage Association
7. insurance companies
8. disintermediation
9. term
10. ration

True–False

1. False	7. False
2. False	8. True
3. True	9. True
4. False	10. True
5. True	11. False
6. True	12. True

Multiple Choice

1. *e*	6. *e*
2. *a*	7. *d*
3. *a*	8. *f*
4. *d*	9. *d*
5. *c*	10. *a*

Answers to Exercise Questions

1. GAAP is what accountants were taught to do in school. RAP is an example of a regulator playing "let's pretend."

2. 1981

3. widening

4. It used to be that even some thrifts with a positive GAAP net worth were closed or merged. By 1984 only a small fraction of those thrifts with a negative GAAP net worth were closed or merged.

5. Knowing only a small percentage of insolvent thrifts will be closed or merged could encourage risk taking by thrifts. Those that are insolvent and still operating are literally investing only other people's money.

6. Higher interest rates hurt thrifts because they specialized in long-term home loans. Their new loans earned the high rates, but the old ones did not. These thrifts had to pay high deposit rates to keep depositors even though the old loans paid lower rates.

7. The decline in GAAP net worth after 1983 was due to loan losses, not interest-rate risk. Some say the new laws allowing thrifts into previously prohibited businesses led to losses as inexperienced thrifts entered highly competitive markets. Others feel thrifts deliberately took higher risks as the threat of FSLIC closing diminished.

8. No. The FSLIC would have needed 15 billion and had only about 6 billion.

9. The decline in interest rates increased the market value of loans.

10. GAAP net worth carries loans at their historical value, not their market value. A $50,000 loan stays a $50,000 loan regardless of interest-rate changes until fully or partially repaid.

11.

Type of Intermediary	Principal Asset(s)	Principal Liability(ies)
Commercial banks	B,C,D,E,I	2,4
Savings and loans	B	2,4
Mutual savings banks	B,F	4
Money-market funds	C,G,H	5
Mutual funds	A,E,F	5
Life insurance companies	B,F	1
Pension funds	A,F	3
Marine, fire, and casualty insurance companies	A,E,F	1
Government agencies	B,D	6
Credit unions	J	5

CHAPTER 6   Capital Markets

Learning Objectives

After studying this chapter, you should be able to

1. distinguish among the different types of securities markets: primary, secondary, open, negotiated, short term, long term.
2. identify the financial instruments that belong to the short-term market and those that belong to the long-term market.
3. explain the functions of the short-term markets.
4. appreciate the linkages among short-term credit instruments.
5. describe the characteristics and functions of the bond, stock, and mortgage markets.
6. use the concept of present value to price stocks and bonds.
7. explain how long-term credit markets are linked.
8. understand what is meant by the expression "term structure of interest rates."
9. understand what factors influence the slope and position of the yield curve.
10. explain the effects on real and nominal wealth of an increase in interest rates, an increase in prices, and an increase in the government's interest-bearing and non-interest-bearing debt.

Key Terms, Concepts, and Institutions

You should be able to define or explain

surplus
deficit
trade credit

mortgage banks
stock retirements
equity capital

primary markets
secondary markets
open markets
negotiated markets
long-term markets
short-term markets
commercial paper
negotiable certificates of
  deposit
investment banking
syndicate
private placement
underwriting

OTC market
FHLBB
FNMA
GNMA
present value
growth stocks
term structure
yield curve
coupon yield
rational expectations
real balance effect
investment value of a stock
holding period yield

Self-Test: Completion

1. Businesses usually run a deficit during _____.

2. Firms that rely too heavily on short-term debt might have
   trouble if market interest rates _____.

3. Firms with stable markets use _____ debt financing than
   cyclically sensitive firms.

4. Existing securities are traded in the _____ markets.

5. _____ refers to promissory notes issued by well-known
   corporations.

6. Large consumer durables are usually financed with _____.

7. The sale of an entire bond issue directly is known as a _____.

8. The greater the term to maturity the _____ the present value.

9. The lower the discount rate the _____ the present value.

10. _____ may act as go-betweens for local developers and
    distant lenders, arranging financing, servicing, and doing other
    legal work associated with a mortgage.

11. _____ was originally a federal agency but is now a private
    corporation.

12. _____ guarantees securities issued by thrift institutions,
    enabling them to offer a (higher/lower) yield.

13. When calculating the present value of a share of stock, a person
    would probably use a _____ discount rate than they would
    use for calculating the present value of a bond.

14. According to the _____ theory, investors are indifferent among different maturity strategies. They would be equally content with one two-year bond or two one-year bonds if the holding period yields were the same.

15. Suppose that the Federal Reserve acts to influence interest rates, and subsequently the Dow Jones Industrial Average drops by 20 points. If analysts attribute the decline in stock prices to the change in interest rates, our analysis suggests that interest rates

must have _____.

Self-Test: True–False

1. Households typically run surpluses.

2. Tax laws encourage firms to obtain funds by issuing new shares of stock.

3. Open markets are markets in which the borrower and lender negotiate directly with each other.

4. The securities traded in the long-term market are far more homogeneous than short-term securities.

5. The prices of long-term bonds will fluctuate more than the prices of short-term bonds for a given change in interest rates.

6. Long-term credit market instruments are close substitutes for each other.

7. The holding-period yield can be different from the coupon yield.

8. According to rational expectations theorists, security prices change very gradually in response to new information.

9. Ceteris paribus, an increase in interest rates decreases wealth.

10. Taxpayers probably discount their future tax liability at the same rate that they assign to the return on bonds.

11. The value of government debt is independent of the price level, since this debt is stated in nominal terms.

12. Investment bankers often work for commercial banks in their trust departments, advising customers as to how they should invest their savings.

13. Most of the trading in the stock market is for existing issues.

14. If short-term rates are greater than long-term rates, the yield curve will slope up.

15. If the current rate of interest is above the rate that investors perceive as "normal" or average, investors will expect short-term interest rates to rise in the future as well.

Self-Test: Multiple Choice

1. A corporation can obtain short-term funds by
   a. issuing commercial paper.
   b. selling CDs.
   c. selling Treasury bills.
   d. borrowing from a bank.
   e. All of the above.

2. All of the following are short-term financial instruments *except*
   a. federal funds.
   b. bank certificates of deposit.
   c. commercial paper.
   d. corporate stock.
   e. Treasury bills.

3. Banks faced with a particularly strong loan demand may
   a. sell Treasury bills.
   b. sell commercial paper.
   c. issue CDs.
   d. buy federal funds
   e. All of the above.

4. Which of the following generally run surpluses?
   a. households
   b. firms
   c. state and local governments
   d. federal government
   e. None of the above.

5. What is the present value of a bond that promises to pay $2,500 in two years if the discount rate of interest is 15 percent?
   a. $1,890.36
   b. $2,173.91
   c. $2,875
   d. $3,306.25
   e. None of the above.

6. Common stock and municipal bonds are competing portfolio pairs for
   a. insurance companies.
   b. wealthy individuals.
   c. commercial banks.

d. pension funds.

e. mutual savings banks.

7. If the Federal Reserve System purchases U.S. government bonds and notes with the intention of injecting seasonally needed funds into the banking network, we would expect
   a. interest rates to increase.
   b. bond prices to increase.
   c. bond prices to decrease.
   d. wealth to increase.
   e. b and d.

8. Purchases and sales of existing government securities are usually made through
   a. investment bankers.
   b. mortgage bankers.
   c. underwriters.
   d. brokers.
   e. securities dealers.

9. Which is likely to fluctuate the most in response to a given change in interest rates?
   a. the price of a 13-week Treasury bill
   b. the price of short-term negotiable certificates of deposits
   c. the price of commercial paper offered by General Motors
   d. the price of federal funds
   e. the price of 20-year bonds issued by Sears, Roebuck, and Company

Topics for Discussion

1. Why do federal government deficits tend to run higher during recessions?

2. Explain how debt financing affects the price of a corporation's stock.

3. Explain why the tax law favors retaining earnings as opposed to issuing new shares of stock to raise funds.

4. Explain how an increase in the yield available on commercial mortgages could drive up the yield on corporate bonds.

5. According to the theory of rational expectations, what factors might an individual take into account in trying to predict future short-term interest rates?

6. Why might a commercial bank consider long-term securities to be poor substitutes for short-term securities?

7. Why are taxpayers unlikely to discount their *future* tax liability for government bonds at the same rate as that *currently* paid on the bonds?

Exercise Questions

1. Figure 6.1 depicts the market for commercial paper. Suppose that Treasury-bill yields increase in anticipation of the Fed tightening up credit. Show on the graph what will happen in the market for commercial paper.

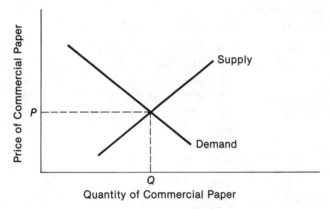

Figure 6.1　The Market for Commercial Paper

The price of commercial paper will _____ (rise/fall).

The yield on commercial paper will _____ (rise/fall).

2. Let C be the dollar amount of a fixed-coupon payment, P_t be the current price of the bond, and P_{t+1} be the price of the bond in the future (its value at maturity or its price when it is sold). For a one-year security, the holding-period yield is given by:

$$\text{Holding-period yield} = \frac{C}{P_t} + \frac{P_{t+1} - P_t}{P_t}.$$

a. What is the holding-period yield for a one-year bond which sells for $990, has a coupon payment of $79.20, and a maturity value of $1,000? _____ percent

b. Is the holding period yield equal to the coupon yield? _____

-49-

c. Suppose the current price of the bond is the same as its maturity value, $1,000. What is the holding-period yield?

_____ percent. Is it the same as the coupon yield?

_____

3. Suppose the holding-period yield on a one-year fixed-coupon bond is 12 percent. You can also buy a two-year fixed-coupon bond with a one-year holding-period yield of 11.5 percent.

a. Which investment would you select?

b. If many other investors followed the same strategy, what would happen to the prices of one-year bonds?
What would happen to the yield on one-year bonds?
What would happen to the prices of two-year bonds?
What would happen to the yield on two-year bonds?

4. In October 1986 the *Wall Street Journal* reported that the Treasury's 7½ percent bonds due 2016 rose to $95^{27}/_{32}$, to yield 7.60 percent. The government's $7^3/_8$ percent notes due 1996 increased to 99½ from $98^{30}/_{32}$, reducing the yield to 7.45 percent. The rate on the latest 13-week Treasury bills slipped to 5.19 percent bid from an average of 5.20 percent. Complete Table 6.1:

Table 6.1 Yield to Maturity for Selected Securities

Type of Security	Years to Maturity (maturity date–1986)	Yield to Maturity (percent)
Treasury bonds, due 2016		
Treasury notes, due 1996		
Treasury bills, 13-week		

Use Figure 6.2 and the information from Table 6.1 to draw a yield curve consistent with the information given above.

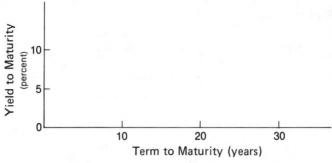

Figure 6.2 A Yield Curve

5. What is the present value of a two-year bond which sells for
$953.125, has a maturity value of $1,000, and pays an annual
coupon of $50? The market rate of interest used for discounting

is 10 percent. _____
Would you buy this bond?

6. Here are two examples of how financial information is reported in
the newspapers. All the quotations are from the *Wall Street
Journal.*

Bond-Market Information

Bonds	Cur Yld	Vol	High	Low	Close	Net Chg.
Sears 10¼88	11	15	96	96	96	$+\frac{1}{8}$

First, you see the name of the company that issued the bond, in
this case Sears. The 10¼ is the coupon yield, and the 88 means the
bond will mature in 1988. Each bond has a face (or par) value
printed right on it. Sears will pay the holder of the bond $1,000 of
principal for each $1,000 of face value when the bond matures in
1988. Sears will also pay 10¼ percent, or $102.50 annually
(usually in semi-annual installments) for each $1,000 of face value.

To conserve space, bond prices are stated as a percentage of 100,
with 100 representing the $1,000 face value. Here, the high, low,
and closing prices for the day were all $960. This closing price was
up ⅛ percent from the previous day's closing price, or $1.25.

The current yield refers to the dollar return per year divided by
the current market price. If the bond pays $102.50 per year and
has a price of $960, the current yield is .1067708, or about 11
percent. Note that the current yield is different from the coupon
yield, since the current price is not equal to the maturity value.

Look at the following quotation:

Bonds	Cur Yld	Vol	High	Low	Close	Net Chg.
GnEl8½04	?	30	76½	76	76½	+¾

a. Who issued the bond?

b. What is the coupon yield? What is the dollar amount (per $1,000 of face value) of the coupon payment?

c. What is the current yield?

d. What was the closing price the day before?

52 Weeks		Stock	Div.	Yld Percent	P-E Ratio	Sales 100s	High	Low	Close	Net Chg.
High	Low									
40	28½	Exxon	3.20	8.7	6	6342	37	36½	36¾	+³⁄₈

Exxon issued this stock, which pays an annual dividend of $3.20. The dividend is compared with the current price to get the current yield. The closing price was 36¾, or $36.75. To get the current yield, we divide $3.20 by $36.75 to get .0870748, or 8.7 percent. The P-E ratio is the price per share divided by the earnings per share. For a given stock price, the lower the P-E ratio, the higher the earnings. The Sales 100s column tells us the number of shares traded on that particular day. The High and Low numbers to the right of the company name tell us the high and low for that day. The High and Low numbers to the left of the company name give the high and low for the stock for the preceding 52 weeks.
Look at the quotation below.

52 Weeks		Stock	Div.	Yld Percent	P-E Ratio	Sales 100s	High	Low	Close	Net Chg.
High	Low									
36⁷⁄₈	21³⁄₈	Avon	2	?	11	1321	24⁷⁄₈	24⁵⁄₈	24³⁄₄	−¹⁄₈

a. What is the name of the issuing company?

b. What is the current yield?

c. Was this stock traded more actively than Exxon on this particular day?

d. What was the lowest price at which you could have bought Avon stock in the last year?

e. What was the closing price the day before?

Answers to Self-Tests

Completion

1. booms
2. rise
3. more
4. secondary
5. commercial paper
6. installment credit
7. private placement
8. less

9. greater
10. Mortgage bankers
11. FNMA
12. GNMA, lower
13. higher
14. expectations
15. risen

True–False

1. True
2. False
3. False
4. False
5. True
6. False
7. True
8. False

9. True
10. False
11. False
12. False
13. True
14. False
15. False

Multiple Choice

1. *e*
2. *d*
3. *e*
4. *a*
5. *a*

6. *b*
7. *e*
8. *e*
9. *e*

Answers to Exercise Questions

1.

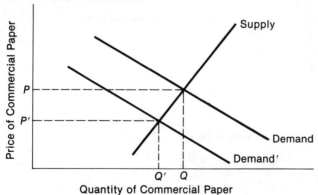

Answer to Figure   The Market for Commercial Paper

fall, rise

2a. Holding-period yield $= C/P_t + (P_{t+1} - P_t)/P_t$
$= \$79.20/\$990 + (\$1,000 - \$990)/\$990$
$= .09 = 9$ percent.

  b. Coupon yield $= C/$Maturity Value $= \$79.20/\$1,000 = .0792 =$
7.92 percent. They are not the same. The holding-period yield
is larger when the price is less than the maturity value.

  c. Holding-period yield $= \$79.20/\$1,000 + (\$1,000 - \$1,000)/$
$\$1,000 = .0792 = 7.92$ percent. The holding-period yield is the
same as the coupon yield if the current price is the same as the
maturity value.

3a. one-year fixed coupon

  b. prices would increase; yield would decrease; prices would decrease;
yield would increase

4.

Type of Security	Years to Maturity (maturity date—1986)	Yield to Maturity (percent)
Treasury bonds, due 2016	30	7.6
Treasury notes, due 1996	10	7.45
Treasury bills, 13-week	¼	5.19

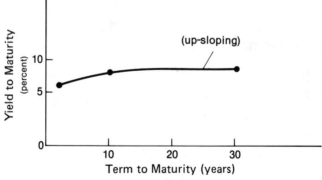

Answer to Figure 6.2 A Yield Curve

5. Present value $= C/(1 + r)^1 + C/(1 + r)^2 + M/(1 + r)^2$
$$= 50/(1 + .10)^1 + 50/(1 + .10)^2 + 1000/(1 + .10)^2$$
$$= \$913.2231 \text{ or } \$913.22.$$
You should not buy the bond—it is overpriced.

6. *Bond-Market Information*

   a. General Electric

   b. 8½ percent; $85

   c. $85/765 = .11111 \doteq 11.1$ percent

   d. $76½ - ¾ = 75¾$, or $757.50

   Stock-Market Information

   a. Avon

   b. $2/24.75 = .080808 = 8.1$ percent

   c. No, Exxon traded 634,200 and Avon traded 132,100 shares. Exxon traded more.

   d. $21^3/_8$, or $21.375

   e. $24¾ + {}^1/_8 = 24^7/_8$, or $24.875

CHAPTER 7   Central Banking

Learning Objectives

After studying this chapter, you should be able to

1. understand the functions of a central bank.

2. understand the historical context of the creation of the Fed in 1913.

3. learn the formal structure of the twelve Federal Reserve District Banks, the Board of Governors, and the Federal Open Market Committee.

4. understand the evolution of informal modes of operation within the Fed.

5. evaluate critically the independence of the Fed.

Key Terms, Concepts, and Institutions

You should be able to define or explain

lender of last resort
central bank
Federal Reserve Bank
Board of Governors
Federal Open Market Committee
discount rate
chore functions

Chairman of the Board
    of Governors
constituency
bureaucracy
independence
open-market operations
political business cycle

Self-Test: Completion

1. In 1913, it was believed that the primary tool of the Fed would be its ability to set the _____.

2. Formally, the six class **A** and class **B** directors are elected by the
   _____. Informally, they are often selected by the _____.

3. The discount rate is set by the _____.

4. Member bank merger applications require the approval of
   _____ or _____.

5. Checks are cleared by the _____.

6. The most powerful single member of the FOMC is the _____.

7. Monetary policy is decided mainly by the _____.

8. Bank holding-company acquisitions are approved by the
   _____.

9. While the Fed does not lend to the government directly, it does
   so indirectly by using the _____ as an intermediary.

10. Legislative recognition of the Fed's control over the money stock
    came with the creation of the _____ in 1935.

11. Banks and the financial community, fixed-income groups, the
    financial press, and the academic economists are all major or
    minor components of the Fed's _____.

12. Fed purchases and sales of securities are called _____.

Self-Test: True–False

1. Congress sets the Fed's budget.

2. The Fed was originally envisioned as a loose confederation of
   twelve regionally dispersed banks each controlled by its own
   Board of Directors.

3. Each president is able to select his own chairman of the Board of
   Governors at the beginning of the president's term of office.

4. The stock of the Fed banks is owned by the member banks and
   pays a 6 percent return.

5. Since 1980 the Fed must charge for the services it provides.

6. The text chapter estimates that the chairman wields about 50
   percent of the authority within the FOMC while the other 50
   percent is held by the other governors.

7. The text chapter presents evidence that the Fed generally shifts course when the presidency changes hands.

8. The president can send a cabinet member to attend the FOMC meetings.

9. The elections of class A and class B directors are vigorously contested.

10. We need a central bank because money will not manage itself.

Self-Test: Multiple Choice

1. When the Fed was created in 1913, its primary function was
   a. control of the money stock.
   b. lender of last resort.
   c. check clearing.
   d. bank examination.
   e. regulation of bank holding companies.

2. Which of the following is an argument for an independent Fed?
   a. Independence strengthens democracy.
   b. Independence allows policy coordination.
   c. Independence may allow the Fed to resist pressure from business and the unemployed to expand the money stock.
   d. The Fed has blundered in the past.
   e. The electorate can be educated to vote intelligently on monetary policy.

3. The Fed pays its bills
   a. through congressional appropriations.
   b. from its earnings on the stock market.
   c. from its ability to create reserves.
   d. from its earnings on securities.
   e. Both c and d.

4. The Fed pursues all of the following goals *except*
   a. a high rate of return for its stockholders.
   b. stable prices.
   c. high employment.
   d. bank safety.
   e. provision of finance to inner cities.

5. Federal Reserve Banks
   a. are commercial banks.
   b. independently set the discount rate for their own districts.

c. make the actual loans to institutions in their district.

d. presidents dominate the FOMC.

e. presidents usually have no influence in the selection of class A and class B directors.

6. The members of the Board of Governors usually serve

a. all of their fourteen-year term.

b. at the pleasure of the president.

c. until replaced by Congress.

d. less than half of their fourteen-year term.

e. until they retire.

7. The influence of the president on the Fed is _____ and

derives from _____.

a. significant, custom

b. significant, law

c. insignificant, custom

d. insignificant, law

8. As a bureaucracy we can expect the Fed to

a. emphasize the long-term impact of policy.

b. openly discuss past errors.

c. share its authority with other agencies and experts.

d. discuss its goals and objectives in concrete and specific terms.

e. avoid conflict with people in power.

9. The primary function of the Fed is now

a. control of the money stock.

b. to earn money for the Treasury.

c. check clearing.

d. bank examination.

e. regulation of bank holding companies.

10. Which of the following Fed banks has a permanent seat on the FOMC?

a. San Francisco

b. Chicago

c. St. Louis

d. New York

e. Richmond

Topics for Discussion

1. What are the goals of a central bank?

2. Describe the degree of congressional control over the Fed. Does Congress control the Fed's budget? Does the ownership of the Fed by its member banks weaken congressional control?

3. Is the Fed independent of the president? What channels of influence exist?

4. Should the Fed be independent? Should the chairman of the Board of Governors serve coterminously with the president? Should the FOMC be required to confer with Congress until a coordinated economic policy is formulated?

5. Should the Fed be required to explain and defend its policies? Would you support a requirement that all deliberations of the FOMC be a matter of public record?

6. Why is the Fed likely to emphasize the near-term effect of policy?

7. Why is the Fed's function as the lender of last resort less significant now than it was in 1913?

8. What functions does the Board of Governors serve independent of its FOMC membership?

9. What is the Fed's constituency? Is it so narrow that the Fed is unlikely to pursue the public interest?

Exercise Questions

These two crossword puzzles are helpful reviews of the details of central banking introduced in this chapter.

Crossword Puzzle One

ACROSS

2. Initially, the Fed was considered a _____ of banks to pool reserves.
4. A condition that bureaucracies suffer from (clue: nearsightedness).
5. What some would like the president's and FOMC chairman's terms to be.
6. The Fed has gradually become more _____.
8. The number of people on the Boards of Directors.
12. An expression of disbelief.
13. Where class B directors could be drawn from.

14. The Fed stands ready and _____ to act as a lender of last resort.
17. _____ of Governors.
20. The number of people on the FOMC.

DOWN

1. Where class B directors could be drawn from.
3. What the Fed ignores, but banks do not.
6. The most powerful member of the FOMC.
7. Stylish.
9. A wine district in Germany.
10. A person, place, or thing.
11. How the Fed feels about the depression.
15. What a central bank is not.
16. What policy decisions rely on.
18. What the Fed tries to avoid.
19. What member banks keep at Fed banks.

Crossword Puzzle Two

ACROSS

1. The group that determines monetary policy.
5. The rate of interest the Fed charges.
6. Where class B directors may be drawn from.
8. Some wish Congress would _____ the Fed's purse strings.
9. As a bureaucracy the Fed might be tempted to take the _____ amendment.
11. University of the Pacific.
12. What the Fed sells on the open market.
13. and 14. The largest Fed bank is in _____ _____.
  (13)   (14)

DOWN

2. The state with two Federal Reserve Banks.
3. Perhaps the Fed should not be independent since it has _____ in the past.
4. The Fed's support group.
5. If reserves _____ the Fed must act as a lender of last resort.
7. It stole Christmas.
9. What the Fed does to fraud.
10. Used by gardeners and firemen.

Answers to Self-Tests

Completion

1. discount rate
2. member banks; President of the Fed bank
3. Board of Governors of the Fed
4. Board of Governors of the Fed; a Reserve Bank
5. Fed Banks
6. Chairman
7. FOMC
8. Board of Governors of the Fed
9. public
10. FOMC
11. constituency
12. open-market operations

True–False

1. False
2. True
3. False
4. True
5. True

6. False
7. True
8. False
9. False
10. True

Multiple Choice

1. *b*
2. *c*
3. *e*
4. *a*
5. *c*

6. *d*
7. *a*
8. *e*
9. *a*
10. *d*

Answer to Crossword Puzzle One

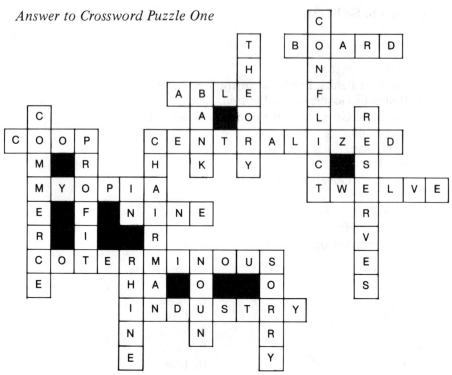

Answer to Crossword Puzzle Two

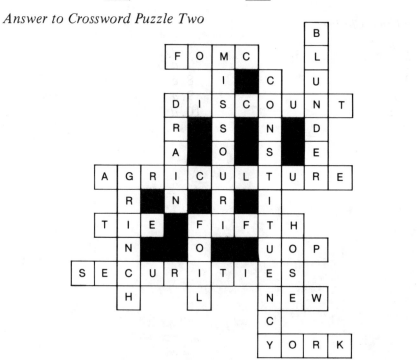

CHAPTER 8   Current Issues in Financial Structure

Learning Objectives

After studying this chapter, you should be able to

1. explain how deposit insurance gives banks and other depository institutions an incentive to take excessive risks.

2. explain how subsidized risk-taking has become a more serious problem since the elimination of Regulation Q.

3. explain the advantages and disadvantages of each of the proposed solutions to the problem of excessive risk-taking by insured depository institutions.

4. explain the pros and cons of separating banking from other lines of business.

5. understand the concept of "competition in laxity."

Key Terms, Concepts, and Institutions

You should be able to define or explain

money brokers
investment banks
"competition in laxity"
capital
"regulatory dialectic"
subsidized risk-taking

secondary capital
crisis in deposit insurance
separation between banking and
    other problems with the
    regulatory structure
lines of business

Self-Test: Completion

1. Under the current system of deposit insurance, the _____

and the _____ subsidize risk-taking by insured depository institutions.

2. _____ _____ break large deposits into units of $100,000 and deposit these $100,000 units in the bank that pays the highest interest rate, regardless of risk.

3. Capital ratios of banks are (higher/lower) now than they were in the 1960s, hence the chance of bank failure is (greater/less).

4. One possible solution to the problem of deposit insurance is to force banks to carry their assets on the books at the actual

   _____ value, rather than at the historical cost of acquisition.

5. The FDIC and FSLIC could (raise/lower) the insurance ceiling to give depositors more incentive to monitor the riskiness of their banks.

6. _____ are firms that help businesses to raise capital by advising them on what stocks and bonds to issue.

7. _____ occurs when the regulatory agencies compete among themselves by limiting the severity of their regulations.

8. The process by which the closing of one loophole creates an incentive to develop others is called the _____.

Self-Test: True–False

1. An advantage of higher capital ratios is that it makes excessive risk-taking a more costly alternative for the insured institution.

2. If a bank fails, depositors bear most of the cost of failure.

3. It is easy for large banks to raise capital by selling stock.

4. Making depositors bear some of the costs of bank failures is more likely to hurt large banks than small banks.

5. Depository institutions may choose which regulatory agencies have jurisdiction over them.

6. Regulatory agencies tend to be overly cautious because they get the blame if they permit banks to do something that causes banks to fail but no credit if they permit banks to do something which ends up to be quite safe.

7. Congress is reluctant to change banking laws for fear of a strong reaction against it on the part of the general public.

8. The votes of those who benefit from a change in the banking laws are likely to just offset the nay votes of those who are hurt by the proposed changes.

9. It is harder now than it was in the past for bank examiners to spot excessive risk-taking.

10. The FSLIC's insurance fund is sufficient to cover the losses of all the thrift institutions that were essentially insolvent in 1986.

Self-Test: Multiple Choice

1. All of the following are factors that may limit risk-taking *except*
   a. the memory of the Great Depression.
   b. the efforts of bank examiners.
   c. reluctance on the part of depositors to bear any of the burden of a bank's failure.
   d. the willingness of bank managers to forgo extra earnings in favor of job security.
   e. All of the above are factors that inhibit risk-taking.

2. Which of the following is an argument against a minimum capital requirement for depository institutions?
   a. Banks that hold too little capital are, in effect, subsidized by those that hold adequate capital.
   b. Banks that hold too much capital have lower profits than those with adequate capital.
   c. It is difficult for banks to raise capital by selling stock because the price of bank stock is so low.
   d. Small banks would have an advantage over large banks in raising capital by issuing bonds.
   e. None of the above.

3. Which of the following is an argument for lowering the deposit insurance ceiling?
   a. Uninsured depositors would be likely to run the bank at the slightest provocation.
   b. Depositors at large banks would have little incentive to monitor the riskiness of their banks, knowing that the FDIC will not let a large bank fail.
   c. Uninsured depositors would force risky banks to pay a higher rate of interest on deposits.
   d. Business depositors always monitor the riskiness of their banks because they hold such large deposits.
   e. Lowered ceilings would encourage large depositors to take advantage of information on the bank's safety, which is currently readily available.

4. Firms in industries that banks wish to enter oppose such entry because
   a. they fear that banks will cut off loans to them in favor of loans to their subsidiaries.
   b. they fear that banks will have an advantage over them because the banks have special privileges from the government.
   c. they fear that banks may take on too much risk and fail.
   d. they argue that banks should not be permitted to engage in outside activities since outside firms are not permitted to engage in banking.
   e. All of the above.
   f. All except d.

5. Subsidized risk-taking has become more of a problem since the elimination of Regulation Q because
   a. risky banks now account for a larger proportion of total deposits.
   b. of the regulatory dialectic.
   c. of the decrease in foreign lending.
   d. of the greater stability of exchange rates.
   e. All of the above.

Topics for Discussion

1. What is it about the current deposit insurance system that encourages depository institutions to take excessive risks?

2. What are the disadvantages of a higher minimum capital ratio for banks?

3. What are the advantages of requiring greater disclosure for banks?

4. What are the advantages of permitting banks to expand into other lines of business?

5. Why doesn't the Congress enact changes in the banking laws in a timely manner?

Exercise Question

The September 8, 1986, edition of the *Wall Street Journal* reported that "the FSLIC sued 27 former officers and directors of the failed Sunrise Savings & Loan Association in Boynton Beach, Fla. (p. 4). The FSLIC, facing a rising number of thrift failures, has been increasingly filing such suits against former officials of failed institutions." What does the FDIC hope to accomplish with these suits?

Answers to Self-Tests

Completion

1. FDIC; FSLIC
2. Money brokers
3. lower; greater
4. market
5. lower
6. Investment banks
7. Competition in laxity
8. regulatory dialectic

True–False

1. True	6. True
2. False	7. False
3. False	8. False
4. False	9. True
5. True	10. False

Multiple Choice

1. *c*
2. *c*
3. *c*
4. *f*
5. *a*

Answer to Exercise Question

The FDIC hopes to (1) bolster its financial strength and (2) put some of the costs of risk-taking on the risk-takers.

CHAPTER 9   The Measurement of Money

Learning Objectives

After studying this chapter, you should be able to

1. understand the empirical and a priori approaches to defining money.

2. come to terms with the problems of defining money in a rapidly changing financial environment.

3. recognize that what we choose to call money may be unimportant but describing the variable the Fed can control to affect nominal income is important.

4. gain some appreciation for the practical difficulties of actually measuring money.

5. assess how reliable money data are.

Key Terms, Concepts, and Institutions

You should be able to define or explain

a priori	Eurodollars
empirical	money-market shares
M-1	repurchase agreements
M-2	weighted aggregate
M-3	standard error
monetary services index	seasonal adjustment

Self-Test: Completion

1. The a priori approach to defining money focuses on money as

   the _____.

2. Dollar-denominated deposits in other countries, principally European countries, are called _____.

3. The approach that focuses on the relationship between money and nominal income is called the _____ approach to the definition of money.

4. If we construct a monetary aggregate that assigns greater weight to assets with lower interest rates the aggregate is called a _____.

5. Credit is not money because credit is not _____.

6. While *M-1* includes most currency, cash in _____ is excluded.

7. All money definitions exclude deposits held by _____.

8. The biggest source of revision of money statistics is the _____ adjustment.

9. If the money growth rate is estimated to be 5 percent and the standard error of estimate is 4 percent then there is a two-thirds chance that the actual growth rate is between _____ percent and _____ percent.

10. Since different financial instruments have different degrees of moneyness, perhaps we ought to construct a money concept that is a _____.

Self-Test: True–False

1. The dispute between the supporters of an a priori definition of money and an empirical definition is a dispute about how the economy operates.

2. An example of a near-money is a credit card line of credit.

3. The weighted aggregate discussed in the text gives a higher weight to assets that pay a higher interest rate.

4. Cash items in the process of collection are deducted from the definition of money on the assumption that those who wrote the checks have already deducted the amount from their records.

5. Interbank deposits are included in the definition of money.

6. Our inability to accurately measure money in the short run means the Fed cannot be expected to achieve precisely the money growth rate it desires.

7. The demand for money always declines at Christmas.

8. The preliminary money-stock data are often revised substantially because the seasonal adjustment is revised substantially.

9. The empirical definition of money tries to identify the money concept that has the greatest influence on income, whether or not that money concept can be controlled by the Fed.

10. The seasonal adjustment can result in higher growth rates of the seasonally adjusted money stock than the unadjusted money stock for every month of a given year.

Self-Test: Multiple Choice

1. Currency is included in
   a. *M-1*.
   b. *M-2*.
   c. *M-3*.
   d. None of the above.
   e. All of the above.

2. Money-market deposit accounts are included in
   a. *M-1*, *M-2*, and *M-3*.
   b. only *M-1*.
   c. only *M-3*.
   d. *M-2* and *M-3*.
   e. only *M-2*.

3. Comparing old and revised monthly growth rates for *M-1* and *M-2* we find that
   a. revisions in *M-2* growth were larger than the revisions in *M-1* growth.
   b. revisions only affected the numbers to the right of the decimal.
   c. revisions in *M-1* growth rates never reversed the sign.
   d. the absolute difference between old and revised *M-1* never exceeded 3 percent.
   e. revisions—especially in 1982—were large enough to significantly affect predictions and policy.

4. Savings deposits are included in *M-2* but not *M-1* because savings deposits
   a. earn a higher rate of interest than the deposits in *M-1*.
   b. are held in thrift institutions.
   c. are not media of exchange.

d. have a penalty for early withdrawal.

e. are not wealth.

5. Assume that last month *M-1* was correctly estimated at $500 billion. This month the true figure for *M-1* is $505 billion but the Fed makes a 1 percent measurement error and believes *M-1* is $510 billion. The true monthly growth rate is 1 percent but the Fed's estimate of the growth rate will be _____ percent representing a measurement error of the growth rate of _____ percent.

    a. 1; 0

    b. 2; 1

    c. 3; 200

    d. 2; 100

    e. 2; 200

6. The biggest source of error in estimating the money stock is

    a. the seasonal adjustment.

    b. adjusting for cash items in the process of collection.

    c. lack of data from smaller institutions.

    d. changes in definitional categories.

    e. reporting errors.

7. In 1986, the year of the data in the text, *M-1* was about

    a. $200 billion.

    b. $600 billion.

    c. $1.5 trillion.

    d. $2.5 trillion.

    e. $3.5 trillion.

8. In 1986 *M-2* was about

    a. $200 billion.

    b. $600 billion.

    c. $1.5 trillion.

    d. $2.5 trillion.

    e. $3.5 trillion.

9. Given that there are different degrees of moneyness it makes sense to

    a. use the inverse of the yield of different forms of money to construct a weighted aggregate.

    b. define money as the inverse of the price level.

    c. measure different kinds of money by how much gold they can buy.

d. give a higher weight to money with a longer time period to maturity.

e. give a higher weight to money with more restrictions on its use.

10. The a priori definition of money focuses on
    a. money as the unit of account.
    b. money as the store of value.
    c. the impact of money on nominal income.
    d. money as the medium of exchange.
    e. All of the above.

Topics for Discussion

1. Why is it important to define money?

2. How would you change the definition of money if it became permissible to write an unlimited number of checks directly against money-market funds?

3. How would you change the definition of money if the government issued a limited number of ration stamps for various commodities? (To buy the good you would need both the stamp and the full cash price.)

4. Argue for a weighted aggregate as the definition of money.

5. Argue against a weighted aggregate as the definition of money.

6. Should the Fed stop seasonally adjusting the monetary aggregates, since the seasonal adjustments are the largest source of revisions?

7. Why do standard errors of estimation for the money growth rate get smaller as the length of the time period gets longer?

Exercise Questions

1. Table 9.1 lists the components of the different monetary aggregates in billions of dollars for May 1986. Your task is to construct the aggregates themselves.

Table 9.1 Components of Monetary Aggregates, May 1986

Currency	175.8
Travelers checks	5.9
Demand deposits	276.7
Other checkable deposits	193.4
Overnight repurchase agreements	49.5
Overnight Eurodollars	17.6
Money-market deposit accounts	530.8
Savings deposits	319.9
Small denomination time deposits	884.7
Money-market mutual funds	
General purpose and broker dealer	193.4
Institution only	76.1
Large denomination time deposits	445.1
Term repurchase agreements	67.7
Term Eurodollars	78.3

Source: Federal Reserve Statistical Release H.6 (508), August 7, 1986. The data are not seasonally adjusted.

Adding up the appropriate components we find that

a. *M-1* is $ _____ billion.

b. *M-2* is $ _____ billion.

c. *M-3* is $ _____ billion.

d. Your figures for *M-2* and *M-3* are slightly higher than the reported figures of $2,638.9 and $3,297.7, respectively. What explains the difference?

2. In Table 9.2 the columns labeled S.A. and N.S.A. contain seasonally adjusted and not seasonally adjusted data.

Table 9.2 Examples of Seasonal Adjustments (in billions of dollars)

	December 1985		April 1986	
	S.A.	N.S.A.	S.A.	N.S.A.
Currency	170.6	173.1	174.4	173.6
Demand deposits	271.5	281.3	275.5	278.7
Other checkable deposits	178.6	180.1	189.9	194.7

Source: Federal Reserve Statistical Release H-6 (508), August 7, 1986.

The seasonal adjustment for December 1985 removes
(*a:* $ _____) billion from currency, (*b:* $_____) billion
from demand deposits, and (*c:* $ _____) billion from other
checkable deposits. Apparently, these are the amounts of additional
currency and checkable deposits the Fed believes people are
holding because of the Christmas season.
   d. Explain the April seasonal adjustment.

Answers to Self-Tests

Completion

   1. medium of exchange
   2. Eurodollars
   3. empirical
   4. monetary services index
   5. wealth
   6. bank vaults
   7. the U.S. government
   8. seasonal
   9. 1; 9
   10. weighted aggregate

True–False

   1. False
   2. True
   3. False
   4. True
   5. False

   6. True
   7. False
   8. True
   9. False
   10. False

Multiple Choice

   1. *e*
   2. *d*
   3. *e*
   4. *c*
   5. *d*

   6. *a*
   7. *b*
   8. *d*
   9. *a*
   10. *d*

Answers to Exercise Questions

1a. $651.8

  b. $2647.7

  c. $3314.9

  d. Some of the categories overlap. The consolidation adjustments remove the double counting. One major source of double counting is money-market mutual funds that are reinvested in some component of *M-3*.

2a. 2.5

  b. 9.8

  c. 1.5

  d. April 15 is the deadline to pay taxes. There is a high volume of check-writing activity at this time and consequently there is an unusually high level of checkable deposits. This has no impact on currency holdings.

CHAPTER 10   The Creation of Money

Learning Objectives

After studying this chapter, you should be able to

1. explain the process of multiple deposit creation and contraction.

2. explain the connection between loan creation and deposit creation.

3. understand how leakages such as excess reserves, deposits into currency, and checkable deposits into time deposits affect the money multiplier and the deposit creation process.

4. use the money multiplier formulas to find *M-1* and *M-2*.

5. state which factors affect the leakage coefficients $e, k,$ and t.

6. explain why, in the absence of Fed action, the money supply would behave procyclically.

7. explain the "New View" of money creation.

Key Terms, Concepts, and Institutions

You should be able to define or explain

reserves (R)
required reserves
excess reserves
T accounts
currency drain
multiple deposit creation
deposit multiplier
reserve-to-demand-deposit ratio

required-reserve-to-demand-deposit ratio (rr)
money multiplier
multiple deposit contraction
time-deposit-to-demand-deposit ratio (t)
required reserve ratio against time deposits (rr_t)

excess-reserve-to-demand-deposit   New View
   ratio (e)   deposits
currency-to-demand-deposit   leakages
   ratio (k)   money supply theory

Extra Help: A Closer Look at the Deposit Multiplier

Why are there so many deposit multipliers, but only one level of deposits? A closer look at the multitude of deposit multipliers shows that they are all variants of one simple relationship, as we will see here.

To find out how deposits, D, and reserves, R, are related, we begin with the identity

$$D = \frac{D}{R} R. \qquad (1)$$

Equation (1) simply says that $D = D$, but we can make the fraction look a lot more like a deposit multiplier by rewriting it as

$$D = \frac{1}{R/D} R. \qquad (2)$$

Because R/D is the mathematical way of phrasing the reserve-to-deposit ratio, we can break down R/D into its two components: the required-reserve-to-deposit ratio, rr, and the excess-reserve-to-deposit ratio, e. So R/D can be rewritten as $rr + e$. Substituting this into Equation (2), we have

$$D = \frac{1}{rr + e} R. \qquad (3)$$

The term $1/(rr + e)$ in Equation (3) is the deposit multiplier for the special case of no currency presented on page 168 of the text. But we have now seen that Equation (3) is always valid, because it is simply a rearranged definition.

Why the need for special cases of the deposit multiplier? Sometimes the information available can be analyzed more quickly with special versions of Equation (3). As the text demonstrates, if the Fed buys $10,000 of securities in the open market and pays for them by check, the check may be deposited, in which case the Fed purchase increases reserves, or the check may be exchanged for cash, in which case the Fed purchase does not change reserves. As the textbook demonstrates, only in the case of no currency can we be sure that reserves change by the full $10,000. Or, if you happen to know the change in reserves, the change in R times $1/(rr + e)$ gives the change in deposits even if currency exists in the system. But we can deal with the existence of currency in a slightly different way. While it is true that we may not know how the $10,000 Fed check will be divided between reserves and currency, the sum of reserves and currency, $R + C$, must rise by $10,000. This suggests changing Equation (1) to

$$D = \frac{D}{R + C} (R + C). \qquad (4)$$

Rearranging as before, we have

$$D = \frac{1}{(R + C)/D} (R + C). \qquad (5)$$

Finally, letting the reserve-to-deposit ratio, R/D, be represented by $rr + e$ as before, and representing the currency-to-deposit ratio, C/D, by k, we have

$$D = \frac{1}{rr + e + k} (R + C). \qquad (6)$$

We can see that Equation (6) is similar to Equation (3). To see how the multiplier in Equation (6) works, suppose again that the Fed writes a check for $10,000 in order to purchase a security on the open market. In this economy $rr = .2$, $e = .05$, and $k = .25$. Since there is currency in the system, Equation (6) is the easiest to apply. The change in deposits equals $1/(.2 + .05 + .25)$ times $10,000. This is $1/(.5)$ times $10,000, or $20,000. (Alternatively, we could use Equation (3) to get the same result. In this economy, we notice that $rr + e = k$, so that the $10,000 is divided equally between reserves and currency. This tells us that the change in reserves is $5,000. Using Equation (3), the change in deposits must be $5,000 times $1/(.2 + .05)$, or $5,000 times 4, which is $20,000.)

Some of the multipliers in the text look more complex than the ones written here. For instance, reserve requirements against different sorts of accounts appear in the multiplier on page 170 of the text as

$$\frac{1}{rr + e + k + t(rr_t)}.$$

The difference between this multiplier and the multiplier in Equation (6) is simply a matter of definition. The Rs above include reserves against all forms of accounts. So the deposit multiplier must include the ratio of reserves against all forms of accounts in R/D. So far, we have used rr to represent the ratio of all required reserves to deposits. The text, on page 170, uses rr to refer only to those required reserves held against demand deposits. If the definition of rr excludes the required reserves held against other forms of accounts, then these other required reserves must be added in.

Equations (3) and (6) demonstrate that the deposit multiplier is always one over the ratio of the multiplicand to deposits. This principle allows us to rewrite deposit multipliers for any special case once we know the multiplicand. For instance, if the multiplicand is excess reserves, the deposit multiplier is $1/e$. (However, the Fed would be severely criticized if it attempted to control deposits by controlling excess reserves since the excess reserve ratio varies a great deal.)

Self-Test: Completion

1. As long as a depository institution has _____ it can create more loans and deposits, should it choose to do so.

2. Multiple deposit creation does not occur if 100 percent reserves are required or if loans are made in _____ only.

3. If the required reserve ratio is 10 percent, and the Fed writes a check for $20,000, the bank that presents the check to the Fed can now make an additional _____ worth of loans should it choose to do so.

4. Frightened Fred withdraws $10,000 from his savings and loan association. If the savings and loan holds no excess reserves and the required reserve ratio is 30 percent then the savings and loan must acquire $_____ in additional reserves.

5. Fred's savings and loan association can get the needed reserves by selling _____ the bank holds, calling in a _____, or borrowing reserves from the Fed.

6. While depository institutions with inadequate reserves would prefer to meet reserve requirements by obtaining more _____, for all depository institutions jointly, this option is controlled by the Fed. Instead, depository institutions may be forced to reduce _____.

7. If tax rates were to increase or if illegal transactions such as drug trafficking and prostitution were to increase then the currency-to-deposit ratio, k, would _____ and the money stock and deposit level would _____ if $R + C$ is held constant.

8. If the Fed increases reserves, the marginal cost of servicing deposits _____.

9. Loans are recorded on the _____-hand side of the bank's T account.

10. Loans are an _____ of the bank because they represent a claim on someone's future assets.

Self-Test: True–False

1. The Fed can control reserves.

2. Since the public decides how much currency to hold, the Fed can not control $R + C$.

3. An increase in the time-deposit ratio, t, reduces $M-1$.

4. To construct $M-1$ we multiply demand deposits by $(1 + k + t)$.

5. Money supply theory allows e, k, and t to vary.

6. An increase in the interest rate tends to reduce e.

7. We can associate $R + C$ with the multiplier $(1/rr)$, even if currency and excess reserves exist.

8. If demand deposits equal $1 billion and $t = 2$, then time deposits equal $2 billion.

9. If $(rr + e) = k$ and $R + C$ is $1 billion, then currency equals $.5 billion.

10. In our system, as the money supply increases, bank loans decrease.

Self-Test: Multiple Choice

Use the following information for Questions 1–6: $(R + C) = \$100$ billion, $k = .25$, $t = .25$, and $rr + e = .15$.

1. Demand deposits equal
   a. $250 billion.
   b. $289.6 billion.
   c. $300 billion.
   d. $320 billion.
   e. $350 billion.

2. Currency, *kD*, equals
    a. $50 billion.
    b. $62.5 billion.
    c. $70 billion.
    d. $75 billion.
    e. $81.6 billion.

3. Total reserves equal
    a. $25 billion.
    b. $32.5 billion.
    c. $37.5 billion.
    d. $50 billion.
    e. $100 billion.

4. Time deposits equal
    a. $50 billion.
    b. $62.5 billion.
    c. $70 billion.
    d. $75 billion.
    e. $81.6 billion.

5. *M-1* is
    a. $200 billion.
    b. $250 billion.
    c. $279.3 billion.
    d. $312.5 billion.
    e. $438.6 billion.

6. *M-2* is
    a. $100 billion.
    b. $200 billion.
    c. $250 billion.
    d. $325 billion.
    e. $375 billion.

7. If business-loan demand increased, then depository institutions

    would probably borrow _____ reserves from the Fed. Unless

    the Fed offset this, the money supply would _____.
    a. more; increase
    b. more; decrease
    c. less; increase
    d. less; decrease
    e. less; not change

8. At Christmastime the public tends to have a _____ currency-to-deposit ratio. This, if $R + C$ is constant, would _____ the money supply.
   a. higher; increase
   b. higher; decrease
   c. lower; increase
   d. lower; decrease
   e. lower; not change

9. If the desired excess reserve ratio is 5 percent, the required reserve ratio is 5 percent, and $10,000 is deposited in Bank A, then Bank A makes a loan of _____ which is deposited in Bank B, which makes a loan of _____.
   a. $9,500; $9,025
   b. $9,000; $8,100
   c. $8,500; $7,225
   d. $9,500; $9,000
   e. $9,000; $8,500

10. According to the New View
   a. the Fed should control $R + C$ and not reserves.
   b. the multiplier approach is too mechanical and leaves out too much that is known about the behavior of depository institutions and the public.
   c. the multiplier approach worked before the 1980 Monetary Control Act but needs a major overhaul now.
   d. the interest rate effects on t and k can be ignored.
   e. banks and the public—not the Fed—control the money supply.

Topics for Discussion

1. In what ways do banks profit from the money creation process?

2. After the Great Depression and the bank runs associated with it, banks maintained unusually large levels of excess reserves. What might explain this?

3. In the mid-1930s the Fed believed the large levels of excess reserves meant the Fed no longer controlled the money supply. They believed any variation in reserve availability would simply be absorbed in a changing excess reserve level. Do you agree?

4. Use the multipliers to explain the seasonal variation in deposits due to an increased currency demand at Christmas. Does this give you an idea about how the seasonal fluctuation could be identified and removed from the data?

5. How might changes in capital requirements affect the multiplier process?

6. How would massive loan losses affect the money creation process?

7. If it were necessary for the Fed to act as a lender of last resort on a massive scale, could it combat inflation at the same time?

Exercise Questions

1. Suppose there is only one kind of depository account with a reserve requirement of 10 percent, no use of currency, and, ultimately, full loaning of excess reserves by banks.

   In this economy, the Fed writes a $100,000 check to a securities dealer named Alice. She deposits the check in her account at Bank A. Record the changes in her bank's T account at this stage.

Bank A

Assets	Liabilities
reserves (a: _____)	deposits (b: _____)

Now excess reserves are (c: _____) and the excess-reserve-to-deposit level is (d: _____). Our formula correctly implies the change in reserves equals the change in deposits since $rr + e =$

(e: _____) + (f: _____) so that the multiplier is

(g: _____).

Bank A loans out the excess (h: $_____) to Allen, an artichoke grower. Allen uses the money to hire Bambi, an independent trucker, to haul the produce to market. Bambi banks at Bank B. Bank B credits Bambi's account and clears the check through the Fed. The Fed transfers reserves from Bank A to Bank B. After the reserve transfer, the T accounts for the two banks look like

Bank A

Assets	Liabilities
reserves (i: _____)	deposits (j: _____)
loans (k: _____)	

Bank B

Assets	Liabilities
reserves (*l:* _____)	deposits (*m:* _____)

Bank B has excess reserves of (*n:* $_____). If this is loaned out, Bank C will find it has (*o:* $_____) it could loan out. The process ends when (*p:* $_____) of new deposits have been created. This can be found by plugging in (*q:* _____) for *e* in our formula. It is also the sum of a geometric progression.

2. Let's adapt the example to allow for currency and excess reserves. Assume *rr* = .1, *e* = .05, and *k* = .1. The Fed check of $100,000 increases *R* + *C* by (*a:* _____). If we multiply this by 1 over

(*b:* _____ + _____ + _____) we have the change in deposits once the banks and the public are again holding the currency and excess reserves they desire. Thus deposits change by

(*c:* _____). Since currency and required reserves both equal 10 percent of deposits, currency must have increased by

(*d:* _____) and required reserves must have increased by

(*e:* _____) while excess reserves at 5 percent of deposits must have increased by (*f:* _____). Notice that their sum is equal to the change in *R* + *C*.

   Now that we know that total reserves have increased by

(*g:* $_____) we can use the multiplier for reserves, which is

1 over (*h:* _____ + _____). Therefore the reserve multiplier is (*i:* _____). Multiplying reserves by the reserve multiplier we find the change in deposits, which is (*j:* _____). Even more simply, we could have multiplied the change in required

reserves of (*k:* _____) times (1/*rr*) and found that deposits

changed by (*l:* _____). So we see that if we know the change in reserves, required reserves, or *R* + *C*, their associated multipliers will all give the change in deposits. However, it is often easier to find the change in *R* + *C* than the changes in any single component.

3. Table 10.1 shows end-of-year figures for reserves, *R* + *C*, and checkable deposits. Calculate the implied deposit multipliers for

reserves, D/R, and for $R + C$, $D/(R + C)$. All figures are in billions of dollars.

Table 10.1 End-of-Year Banking Data, 1979–1982

	1979	1980	1981	1982
R	40.66	40.66	40.59	41.85
$R + C$	162.5	162.5	173.8	179.3
D	287.1	302.4	322.4	328.7
D/R	_____	_____	_____	_____
$D/(R + C)$	_____	_____	_____	_____

a. What can account for the increase in the multipliers for both $R + C$ and reserves for the period 1979 to 1980? How does this square with what you know about the Monetary Control Act of 1980?

b. Explain how the multiplier for $R + C$ could be almost constant from 1980 to 1981 while the multiplier for reserves rose in the same period.

Answers to Self-Tests

Completion

1. excess reserves
2. cash
3. $18,000
4. $7,000
5. securities; loan
6. reserves; deposits
7. increase; decrease
8. declines
9. left
10. asset

True–False

1. True
2. False
3. True
4. False
5. True

6. True
7. False
8. True
9. True
10. False

Multiple Choice

1. *a*	6. *e*
2. *b*	7. *a*
3. *c*	8. *b*
4. *b*	9. *b*
5. *d*	10. *b*

Answers to Exercise Questions

1*a.* 100,000
  b. 100,000
  c. 90,000
  d. .9
  e. .1
  f. .9
  g. 1
  h. 90,000
  i. 10,000

  j. 100,000
  k. 90,000
  l. 90,000
  m. 90,000
  n. 81,000
  o. 72,900
  p. 1,000,000
  q. 0

2*a.* 100,000
  b. .1 + .05 + .1
  c. 400,000
  d. 40,000
  e. 40,000
  f. 20,000

  g. 60,000
  h. .1 + .05
  i. 6.67
  j. 400,000
  k. 40,000
  l. 400,000

3.

	1979	1980	1981	1982
D/R	7.06	7.44	7.94	7.85
$D/(R + C)$	1.77	1.86	1.86	1.83

    a. The reserve-to-deposit level must have fallen. The 1980 law set universal reserve requirements for member and nonmember institutions. These requirements were lower than the old requirements for member banks but higher than the old requirements set for nonmembers. Under the law, member banks have phased in the new requirements faster than nonmembers. As a result, for the first few years after 1980 average reserve requirements fell.

    b. The multiplier for $R + C$ could fall as the currency-to-deposit ratio rose. This would not affect the reserves multiplier.

CHAPTER 11 Bank Reserves and Related Measures

Learning Objectives

After studying this chapter, you should be able to

1. understand the mechanism by which the Fed controls the base, reserves, and the money supply.

2. recognize that while actions by the Treasury, the public, banks, and foreign central banks all affect the various reserve measures the Fed is able to offset these effects.

3. understand why the Fed's control over the base is not perfect in the short run.

Key Terms, Concepts, and Institutions

You should be able to define or explain

borrowings from the Fed
float
free reserves
unborrowed reserves

unborrowed base
base
other Fed liabilities
adjusted base

Self-Test: Completion

1. Bad weather can increase reserves by increasing _____.

2. If the Fed intervenes in foreign-exchange markets to buy Swiss francs, then the Fed check _____ both reserves and the base.

3. Total reserves less reserves held at the Fed equals _____.

4. As the Fed clears a check, sometimes the reserves of the bank presenting the check are increased before the reserves of the bank it is drawn on are reduced. This is called _____.

5. If borrowed reserves increase, the base _____ while the unborrowed base _____.

6. As average reserve requirements fall, the adjusted base _____.

7. The money multiplier for the adjusted base has been declining over time because of an increase in _____ holdings.

8. Excess reserves minus borrowed reserves equals _____.

9. Those factors that can change reserves but are beyond the Fed's control are called _____.

Self-Test: True–False

1. An increase in free reserves means deposits have increased.

2. The money stock increases when the Fed buys paper clips.

3a. An increase in Treasury currency held by the public can affect the accounts in three places. First, Treasury currency outstanding rises. By itself this increases reserves.

 b. Next, currency held by the public rises and this reduces reserves.

 c. Finally, if the treasury deposits the check written by John Q. Public in their account at the Fed, then Treasury deposits at the Fed increase. This reduces reserves.

 d. The net effect is a reduction of reserves.

4. If a new member bank buys Fed stock, reserves fall.

5. When the Treasury shifts tax funds that have been collecting in depository institutions to its Fed account, reserves increase.

6. Unless the money multiplier is a constant, the Fed cannot control the money supply by controlling reserves.

7. The money multipliers for the adjusted base have been rising steadily.

8. Monetary policy can still be expansionary even if the base has not changed.

9. If depository institutions rapidly repay any borrowed reserves rather than use them to finance additional loans, then deposit creation depends more on unborrowed reserves than total reserves.

Self-Test: Multiple Choice

Table 11.1 Selected Fed Data, May 7, 1986 (millions)

Reserves held with Fed banks	$28,676
Total reserves including cash	$48,500
Required reserves	$47,612
Borrowings from the Fed	$981
Currency in circulation	$195,151

Source: Federal Reserve Bulletin, August 1986.

1. According to Table 11.1, on May 7, 1986, excess reserves were
   a. $19,824 million.
   b. $888 million.
   c. $93 million.
   d. $1,566 million.
   e. $242,670 million.

2. According to Table 11.1, on May 7, 1986, unborrowed reserves were
   a. $888 million.
   b. $47,519 million.
   c. $242,670 million.
   d. $243,651 million.
   e. $19,824 million.

3. According to Table 11.1, on May 7, 1986, the base was
   a. $888 million.
   b. $19,824 million.
   c. $47,519 million.
   d. $243,651 million.
   e. $242,670 million.

4. According to Table 11.1, on May 7, 1986, vault cash was
   a. $888 million.
   b. $47,519 million.

c. $242,670 million.
d. $243,651 million.
e. $19,824 million.

5. According to Table 11.1, on May 7, 1986, the unborrowed base was
   a. $888 million.
   b. $47,519 million.
   c. $242,670 million.
   d. $243,651 million.
   e. $19,824 million.

6. According to Table 11.1, on May 7, 1986, free reserves were
   a. -$93 million.
   b. $888 million.
   c. $19,824 million.
   d. $444 million.
   e. $47,519 million.

7. An increase in other Federal reserve liabilities
   a. increases reserves because the Fed had to buy the liabilities.
   b. increases reserves because Fed liabilities are currency and currency is reserves.
   c. decreases reserves because this represents assets acquired but not paid for.
   d. decreases reserves because it is a technical adjustment to avoid double counting Treasury currency.
   e. does not change reserves.

8. When the Fed writes a check which of the following increases?
   a. reserves
   b. unborrowed reserves
   c. the base
   d. the unborrowed base
   e. All the above.

9. An increase in currency in circulation _____ reserves and
   _____ the base.
   a. increases; increases
   b. increases; decreases
   c. decreases; increases
   d. decreases; decreases
   e. decreases; does not change

10. Free reserves are
    a. interest-free loans from the Fed to unprofitable institutions.
    b. reserves that the institution is free to use to make loans.
    c. excess reserves less borrowed reserves.
    d. always positive.
    e. always positive when deposits are increasing.

Topics for Discussion

1. On June 14, 1983, the *Wall Street Journal* reported that news of open-market sales of securities had sent jitters through the financial community on June 13 until news of large Fed loans to troubled Seattle First National Bank were announced. Analysts then concluded the reserve draining operation was a technical adjustment and not a sign of a policy change. Explain.

2. How is it possible for free reserves to fall and reserves to rise?

3. Why does the Fed prefer to watch unborrowed reserves and the unborrowed base?

Exercise Questions

1. Use the changes in various Fed accounts listed in Table 11.2 to calculate the change in reserves from August 6 to August 13, 1986.

Table 11.2 Weekly Published Federal Reserve Data—Member Bank Reserve Changes, August 6–13, 1986 (millions of dollars)

Purchases of U.S. government securities, securities of U.S. government agencies, and acceptances	+550
Borrowings from the Fed	+107
Float	−907
Other Fed assets	+298
Gold stock	—
SDR certificates	—
Treasury currency outstanding	+14
Currency in circulation	+779
Treasury cash holdings	—
Treasury, foreign, and other deposits with F. R. banks	−13
Other Fed liabilities	+12

Source: *Wall Street Journal*, August 15, 1986, p. 18.

2. Derive multipliers for the nonborrowed base and nonborrowed reserves. Use *b* to represent the borrowed-reserve-to-demand-deposit ratio. (See Extra Help Section in Chapter 10.)

Answers to Self-Tests

Completion

1. float
2. increases
3. vault cash
4. float
5. increases; does not change
6. rises
7. currency
8. free reserves
9. operating factors or market factors

True–False

1. False	4. True
2. True	5. False
3*a*. True	6. False
b. True	7. False
c. True	8. True
d. True	9. True

Multiple Choice

1. *b*	6. *a*
2. *b*	7. *c*
3. *d*	8. *e*
4. *e*	9. *e*
5. *c*	10. *c*

Answers to Exercise Questions

1. Draw a line between Treasury currency outstanding and currency in circulation. Add up the numbers above the line and subtract the numbers below the line. Reserves decreased by $716 million.

2. The multipliers are

$$\frac{1}{rr + e + k - b} \text{ and } \frac{1}{rr + e - b}.$$

Notice that the denominators are the ratios of the non-borrowed base to deposits and nonborrowed reserves to deposits. Focusing on either of these measures allows bank borrowing to affect the multiplier.

CHAPTER 12　The Determinants of Aggregate Demand

Learning Objectives

After studying this chapter, you should be able to

1. use either the Keynesian or monetarist approach to explain variations in aggregate demand.

2. explain how the Cambridge and quantity theory approaches lead to different variables as the causes of fluctuations in aggregate demand.

3. use a 45-degree diagram to illustrate the impact of changes in investment, consumption, and government tax and spending policies on aggregate demand and production.

4. explain how the interaction of the multiplier and accelerator could lead to economic instability.

5. explain the user cost of capital.

Key Terms, Concepts, and Institutions

You should be able to define or explain

Keynesian approach
monetarist approach
consumption
investment
government spending
net exports
velocity (or income velocity)
real vs. nominal income
quantity theory of money
Cambridge equation

transactions velocity
autonomous consumption
marginal propensity to consume
disposable income
permanent income
user cost
depreciation
capital coefficient
accelerator
investment multiplier

Self-Test: Completion

1. Keynesians link aggregate demand to _____ while

   monetarists link aggregate demand to _____.

2. In the Keynesian approach, output retained by business is

   called _____. (Notice that this excludes bonds and stocks,
   included in the common usage of the term.)

3. Income after personal taxes have been deducted is called

   _____.

4. The _____ theory argues that consumption depends on
   anticipated income as well as current income.

5. The user cost of capital has four components. They are

   _____, which reflects the change in the value of capital

   over time; _____, which reflects the cost of borrowed funds;

   _____, which compensates for uncertainty; and _____,
   which is wholly dependent on government decisions.

6. Investment less depreciation is _____.

7. Firms can raise money by selling their accounts receivable; this is

   called _____.

8. Exports less imports are _____.

9. Higher prices increase _____ income but not _____
   income.

10. The interaction of the multiplier and the _____ could cause
    income to shoot up or down dramatically.

11. If government spending rises by $1 billion, the marginal propensity
    to consume, c, is .75, and investment is unchanged, then income

    should rise by _____ billion.

Self-Test: True–False

1. Most economists attribute fluctuations in nominal and real GNP
   primarily to fluctuations in the capacity to produce.

2. Income velocity measures the number of times a dollar is spent,
   on average, within a given period.

3. Transactions velocity includes spending on intermediate products and is therefore greater than income velocity.

4. $Y = C + I + G + X$ because all production, Y, must eventually end up in the hands of households, C, businesses, I, government, G, or foreigners, X.

5. If actual investment is greater than desired investment, then there is an unintended depletion of inventories.

6. It may be important to include both current and permanent income in the consumption function if households cannot borrow enough against their future income.

7. Capital is a flow, whereas investment is a stock.

8. A firm's net investment must be positive just to maintain its current output.

9. The economy should be more stable if consumption depends on permanent income rather than on current income.

10. The investment multiplier applies only to investment and not to changes in government spending.

11. Higher taxes reduce the multiplier because each dollar earned has a smaller impact on disposable income and the next round of spending.

Self-Test: Multiple Choice

1. The Cambridge equation and the quantity equation are different because
   a. the Cambridge k and income velocity often move independently of each other.
   b. the Cambridge k emphasizes the mechanics of transactions rather than human decision-making.
   c. the Cambridge k leads us to consider income and the opportunity cost of holding money as important determinants of aggregate demand.
   d. the Cambridge k leads us to consider technology and the speed with which transactions can be conducted as important determinants of aggregate demand.
   e. the Cambridge approach denies the importance of money as a factor affecting aggregate demand.

2. Compared to income velocity, transactions velocity
   a. is more commonly used because we have better data on transactions than on income.
   b. is lower because much is generated without transactions.
   c. is only a tautology. No assumptions need be added to income velocity to make it a useful theory.
   d. focuses on the less interesting variable (transactions).
   e. is less heavily affected by stock market sales and used car sales.

3. We expect savings to fall and consumption to rise if
   a. the middle aged become a larger share of the population.
   b. wealth increases.
   c. a religious movement that denounces material possessions expands.
   d. social security programs are repealed.
   e. people become convinced their income will fall.

4. Higher real interest rates affect consumption by
   a. rewarding savings more heavily.
   b. increasing the value of securities that households hold.
   c. increasing the household's liquidity.
   d. reducing the opportunity cost of purchasing consumer durables.
   e. relaxing credit rationing.

5. The user cost of capital increases if
   a. over time the firm's ratio of debt to net worth falls.
   b. the breakdown of international trade agreements increases uncertainty.
   c. bond prices rise.
   d. stock prices rise.
   e. the government increases tax breaks for investment.

6. The acceleration principle results from the fact that
   a. investment by one firm leads to increased demand for other firms' products and more investment by other firms.
   b. the capital stock is generally several times output, so that an increase in desired output leads to a multiplied increase in desired capital.
   c. business expansion increases employment and consumption.
   d. once stock prices begin to fall they are expected to fall so investors sell them.
   e. success by one firm increases optimism.

7. Accelerator effects may not be particularly strong because
   a. rapidly expanding the capital stock is more expensive than a slow expansion.

b. expansions by several firms simultaneously can significantly increase the cost of capital goods.

c. even if current output rises significantly, anticipated output may not change much.

d. the investment process can disrupt the firm's other activities, especially if the firm embarks on a crash program.

e. All of the above.

8. The economy will tend to be more stable if
   a. the capital coefficient is large.
   b. the multiplier is large.
   c. income increases are assumed to be permanent.
   d. our ability to predict the future yield of investment improves.
   e. consumption depends only on current income.

9. According to the quantity theory equation,
   a. if the money stock rises and velocity is constant then income rises but not prices.
   b. if money and velocity are constant, an increase in income implies a reduction in prices.
   c. if the stock of money rises and velocity declines, we do not know how prices and income vary.
   d. if velocity and income are constant then doubling the money supply must double prices.
   e. All but *a.*

10. Investment increases if
    a. the risk premium increases.
    b. anticipated sales increase.
    c. debt to net worth ratios increase.
    d. interest rates increase.
    e. All of the above.

Topics for Discussion

1. From the Keynesian approach we know that increases in government spending increase income. For the quantity theory to be consistent with this, income velocity must rise as government spending increases. Why would it?

2. How do you think the baby boom of the 1950s affected consumption? The baby boomers are in their mid-thirties now, so should consumption be a high or a low fraction of income?

3. The Keynesian model assumes that when firms find they cannot sell all that they intended, they cut production. Do you think firms do this? Or do they cut prices or launch an advertising campaign?

4. Why do interest rates tend to rise as customers and businesses regain confidence and spend their way out of a recession?

5. Why do shifts in aggregate demand generate further shifts in the same direction? Try to think of both real and monetary effects.

Exercise Questions

1a. Imagine an economy made up of 40 workers. Production uses only labor and there are no bosses, profit, or government. Each employed worker receives $50 a day. All workers spend $10 a day plus half of whatever they earn. What is the consumption function for this economy?

b. The production facilities are run by a workers' committee. (This is done for simplicity.) There are 12 production lines capable of employing 4 people each for a grand total of 48 possible jobs. The worker's committee has decided to invest $400 each period. Fill in Table 12.1. Income is equal to the number of people hired times $50. Consumption is half of income plus $400. Planned investment is $400. Calculate consumption plus planned investment, $C + I$. This is aggregate demand. Compare this to production. (Production equals income because production generates income for someone.) Now subtract demand from production, $Y - (C + I)$. This is unplanned inventory accumulation. If unplanned inventory accumulation is negative, more will be hired. If unplanned inventory accumulation is positive, fewer will be hired.

Table 12.1 Income, Consumption, and Employment Figures

Number hired	Income	Consumption	$C + I$	Unplanned inventory accumulation	Are more or fewer hired?
40					
36					
32					
28					
16					
0					

2. Draw the $C + I$ and 45-degree lines that correspond to the economy above in Figure 12.1. To plot the $C + I$ line, first plot the consumption and income pairs you calculated in Question 1 as the consumption function, then add $400 to this for the $C + I$ line.

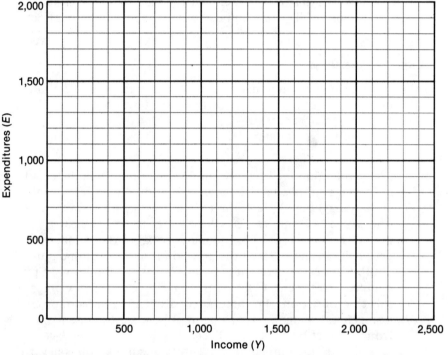

Figure 12.1 The 45-Degree Diagram for the Workers' Economy

3. Confirm that the equilibrium income levels you found in Questions 1 and 2 above are correct by multiplying planned investment plus autonomous consumption by the investment multiplier.

4. Use diagrams like the one you constructed above to illustrate the effects of
   a. higher taxes.
   b. higher government spending.
   c. lower investment.

5. How must the changes in Question 4 change income velocity if the quantity theory and the income-expenditure approach are consistent? How do you know?

Answers to Self-Tests

Completion

1. income; the money supply
2. investment
3. disposable income
4. permanent income
5. depreciation; interest rate; risk premium; tax effect
6. net investment
7. factoring
8. net exports
9. nominal; real
10. accelerator
11. $4

True–False

1. False	7. False
2. False	8. False
3. True	9. True
4. True	10. False
5. False	11. True
6. True	

Multiple Choice

1. *c*	6. *b*
2. *d*	7. *e*
3. *b*	8. *d*
4. *a*	9. *e*
5. *b*	10. *b*

Answers to Exercise Questions

1a. $C = .5Y + \$400$.

Table 12.1 Income, Consumption, and Employment Figures

Number hired	Income	Consumption	$C + I$	Unplanned inventory accumulation	Are more or fewer hired?
40	$2,000	$1,400	1800	$200	Fewer
36	1,800	1,300	1700	100	Fewer
32	1,600	1,200	1600	0	No change
28	1,400	1,100	1500	-100	More
16	800	800	1200	-400	More
0	0	400	800	-800	More

2.

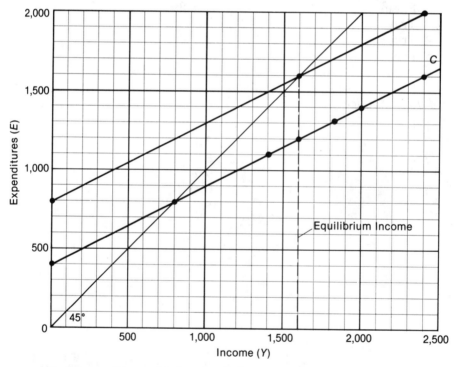

Answer to Figure 12.1 The Workers' 45-Degree Diagram

3. $(400 + 400)(1/.5) = 1600$

    4a. An increase in taxes reduces disposable income and consumption. Therefore the $C + I$ line shifts down and equilibrium income falls.

    b. An increase in government spending increases demand. Demand is now $C + I + G$. Equilibrium income increases.

    c. A reduction in investment reduces $C + I$ and equilibrium income falls.

5. The quantity theory equation is $MV = PY$. In the income-expenditure exercises above, P and M are assumed constant. If P and M are constant but Y changes, then V must change in the same direction to preserve the equality. Parts a and c result in a lower income level so velocity must have declined, while in part b income increased so velocity must have increased. Why velocity changes will be explained in Chapter 16.

CHAPTER 13   The Interest Rate

Learning Objectives

After studying this chapter, you should be able to

1. explain why interest rates are important.
2. use both the loanable funds theory and the liquidity preference theory to explain how interest rates are determined.
3. explain the time path of interest rates given an increase in the supply of money, and explain the sensitivity of the time path to expected inflation and price flexibility.
4. explain how taxes and the expected inflation rate affect nominal interest rates.

Key Terms, Concepts, and Institutions

You should be able to define or explain

loanable funds theory
capital inflows
inflation premium
expected real rate
completely flexible prices
rational expectations

liquidity preference theory
efficient markets theory
Fisher effect
Darby effect
adaptive expectations
liquidity effect

Self-Test: Completion

1. The three sources of loanable funds are real _____, and real _____ _____, and the real _____ _____.

2. If the dollar is depreciating at 4 percent a year compared to the Japanese yen, and if unrestricted Japanese securities pay 6 per-

cent a year, then comparable U.S. securities would have to pay

about _____ percent to compete.

3. According to the _____ theory, markets set prices that already take all available information into account.

4. The nominal interest rate can be broken into two components,

the expected _____ of interest and expected _____.

5. If anticipated inflation is 8 percent, the nominal interest rate is 12 percent, and the tax rate is 50 percent, then the real after-tax

rate of interest is _____ percent.

6. An increase in the money supply may reduce nominal interest rates, at least until prices and expectations begin to adjust. This is

called the _____.

7. A professor is 10 minutes late for the beginning of class and announces he has an immediately preceding class across campus.

A student using _____ expectations may allow himself an additional 5 minutes before coming to class the next day, while a

student using _____ expectations may take the full 10 minutes.

8. If people are constantly searching for models that predict events, and throw out those that lead to systematic error, then they are

using a _____ expectations approach.

9. If announced increases in the supply of money had no impact on employment or output, and led to suddenly higher inflation and nominal interest rates, this would be evidence that the economy

had _____ prices and _____ expectations.

10. The _____ effect explains the effect of taxes on real interest rates.

Self-Test: True–False

1. Real savings by households exceed the real savings by firms.

2. A higher rate of interest makes future goods more expensive compared to current goods.

3. An increase in the demand for money can increase the demand for loanable funds, as businesses or households borrow to acquire the additional cash.

4. An increase in foreign interest rates would shift the supply of loanable funds to the left, and lead to higher interest rates here.

5. Even with completely flexible prices, involuntary equilibrium unemployment is possible.

6. If expected inflation is 7 percent and the nominal interest rate is 10 percent then the expected real rate of interest, ignoring potential tax effects, is 17 percent.

7. Adaptive expectations can be explained as expectations that are an average of past experience. If inflation were to suddenly increase, it would take some time before the expectation caught up with reality.

8. Higher money growth cannot lead to lower nominal interest rates except for a short time period. However, the inflation created may reduce after-tax real interest rates.

9. Even if formal and informal contracts exist that make prices slow to adjust, the rational expectation theory implies that money has no impact on real interest rates or output.

10. A comparison of annual money growth rates and annual averages of the Treasury-bill rate reveals a strong liquidity effect.

11. For much of the 1970s, the real after-tax interest rate was negative.

Self-Test: Multiple Choice

1. An increase in the real money supply increases real loanable funds because
   a. a higher money supply is a reflection of higher government lending.
   b. in our system bank loan creation and money creation are intertwined.
   c. as people expect more inflation they are more willing to make loans.
   d. there is no difference between loans and money.
   e. Both a and b.

2. An increase in real savings increases the supply of loanable funds and
   a. increases the demand for money so the two theories conflict.
   b. decreases money demand because the higher savings reduce interest rates and therefore reduce money demand.
   c. increases money demand as the lower interest rate boosts investment and income.
   d. decreases money demand as higher savings reduce both consumption and aggregate demand. With lower demand, production and income fall, reducing the demand for money.
   e. decreases money demand as those with more wealth desire less money.

3. An increase in investment
   a. increases the demand for loanable funds and increases the money supply.
   b. increases the supply of loanable funds and increases the money supply.
   c. increases the supply of loanable funds and increases the demand for money.
   d. increases the demand for loanable funds and increases money demand.
   e. increases the demand for loanable funds and decreases money demand.

4. An increase in real income
   a. could either increase or decrease the supply of loanable funds but clearly increases money demand without changing money supply.
   b. increases money demand but increases the supply of loanable funds.
   c. increases money supply as people earn more.
   d. increases the demand for loanable funds and decreases money demand.
   e. can occur only if interest rates decline and allow more investment.

5. If the Fed were to buy government securities on the open market we would expect the supply of loanable funds to _____, the supply of money to _____, and the interest rate to _____.
   a. increase; increase; increase.
   b. increase; increase; decrease.
   c. decrease; increase; decrease.
   d. decrease; decrease; increase.
   e. increase; decrease; increase.

6. An increase in the marginal productivity of capital _____ the demand for loanable funds, _____ money demand, and _____ interest rates.
   a. increases; increases; increases.
   b. increases; increases; decreases.
   c. decreases; increases; decreases.
   d. decreases; decreases; increases.
   e. increases; decreases; increases.

7. If the money supply rises in a completely price flexible economy then output and employment _____, prices _____, and the real money supply _____.
   a. increase; increase; increases.
   b. do not change; increase; increases.
   c. do not change; increase; does not change.
   d. increase; increase; decreases.
   e. increase; increase; does not change.

8. If expectations are adaptive and prices are slow to adjust, then an increase in the supply of money will, for a limited time, _____ the expected real interest rate, _____ employment and output, and _____ the real money supply.
   a. increase; increase; increase.
   b. not change; increase; increase.
   c. not change; increase; not change.
   d. decrease; increase; increase.
   e. decrease; increase; not change.

9. Inflation can affect the real interest rate because
   a. inflation increases uncertainty and thereby increases savings and reduces investment.
   b. inflation increases wealth so people save less.
   c. inflation reduces the corporate tax burden.
   d. assuming flexible prices, inflation increases income and leads to higher investment through an accelerator effect.
   e. All of the above.

Topics for Discussion

1. Why have interest rates become more variable?

2. You will find "Credit Markets" as a "Today's Contents" heading on the bottom of the first page of today's *Wall Street Journal*. Turn to the page indicated and interpret the day's events with either the loanable funds or liquidity preference theory.

3. The text discusses the effects of an increase in money growth. What would happen to the time path of interest rates, output, and inflation if the Fed reduced money growth? How does this compare with the U.S. economy in the early 1980s? (See the endpapers of the text.)

Exercise Questions

1. The *Wall Street Journal* reported on August 4, 1986, that the Federal government's massive borrowing needs would dominate the credit markets. Analysts wondered if the Japanese would continue to acquire new government issues, as they had in May, given the slide in the value of the dollar. Your task is to interpret these events using either the loanable funds or the liquidity preference theory. First, determine which theory is easiest to use. Then describe these events as a shift in one curve and uncertainty over the slope of the other.

2. The same issue of the *Wall Street Journal* indicated that bond prices for both public and private issues fell in anticipation of the Treasury auction. Why would *privately* issued bond prices fall *before* the auction?

3. On August 5, 1986, the *Wall Street Journal* reported an OPEC agreement to restrict production and boost oil prices and new regulations issued by the Japanese government that made it easier for Japanese insurance companies and trust banks to acquire U.S. securities. How do you think the credit markets responded? Why?

Answers to Self-Tests

Completion

1. savings; capital inflow; money supply.
2. 10
3. efficient markets
4. real rate; inflation
5. −2
6. liquidity effect

7. adaptive; rational
8. rational
9. flexible; rational
10. Darby

True–False

1. False
2. False
3. True
4. True
5. False (Although some theoretical models do exist with
   carefully defined involuntary
   unemployment at a flexible
   price equilibrium.)

6. False
7. True
8. True
9. False
10. False
11. True

Multiple Choice

1. *b*
2. *d*
3. *d*
4. *a*
5. *b*

6. *a*
7. *c*
8. *d*
9. *a*

Answers to Exercise Questions

1. The loanable funds theory is easiest because the capital inflow
   is part of the supply of loanable funds and the government
   borrowing directly affects the demand for loanable funds. The
   increased government borrowing clearly shifts the demand for
   loanable funds toward higher interest rates. The uncertainty
   concerning the response of the Japanese is uncertainty over the
   slope of the supply of loanable funds. If the Japanese invest
   heavily in response to a small interest rate increase, the supply of
   funds is elastic or flat. If uncertainty over exchange rates has
   frightened off the Japanese, then the interest rates will have to
   rise more to entice more domestic and foreign lenders to enter
   the market, and the supply of loanable funds is inelastic or steep.

2. If you expect higher interest rates you expect lower bond prices,
   so sell your bonds before the price falls. But, selling bonds
   reduces bond prices. Privately issued securities are affected
   because people shift from private to public issues as the yield on
   public issues increases.

3. The OPEC agreement led to concern over higher inflation and therefore lower bond prices (the Fisher effect). The easing of investment restrictions was expected to increase the supply of loanable funds, leading to lower interest rates and higher bond prices. Since the two effects offset each other, the net effect is difficult to determine. In fact, by the end of the day, bond prices were almost unchanged.

CHAPTER 14   The Demand for Money

Learning Objectives

After studying this chapter, you should be able to

1. state the connection between the demand for money and the interest rate.

2. explain the connection between money demand and income velocity.

3. use the velocity connection to explain why monetary policy requires good information on both the supply and demand for money.

4. differentiate between transaction, speculative, and precautionary demands for money.

5. explain why both the interest rate and the cost of investing affect the transaction demand for money.

6. apply standard demand theory to the demand for money.

7. explain why the failure of estimated money demand functions to predict well into the 1970s and early 1980s complicated the Fed's job.

Key Terms, Concepts, and Institutions

You should be able to define or explain

transactions demand	precautionary demand
speculative demand	the cost of investing
net interest forgone	substitutes
complements	demand function
the case of the missing money	statistical demand function

Self-Test: Completion

1. If the public holds large volumes of Treasury bills and money-market accounts, the cost of selling assets will be low. These are examples of _____ assets.

2. Someone who converts all his monthly income to cash and spends it gradually over the month may be ignoring the potential benefits of _____.

3. Money held in the event of an unforeseen expense is called a _____ demand for money.

4. Money held to meet anticipated expenses is called a _____ demand for money.

5. In general, the demand for a good depends on its own price, the prices of _____, and the prices of _____.

6. In general, demand depends not only on prices but also on _____ and _____.

7. If the demand for money were to increase because people were more confident about the future we would say demand shifted due to a change in _____. (List one of the determinants of money demand.)

8. An increase in anticipated stock returns would shift money demand through a change in _____. (List one of the determinants of money demand.)

9. Payment of interest on checkable deposits would change money demand by changing _____. (List one of the determinants of money demand.)

10. Some economists have tried to solve the case of the missing money by adding _____ to measure cash management by firms or _____ to measure stock market returns.

Self-Test: True–False

1. Per capita money holdings are larger than per capita monthly income.

2. The higher the cost of investing and later disinvesting, the lower money holdings will be.

3. The trouble involved in acquiring and later liquidating securities rises in proportion to the amount involved.

4. The marginal benefit of precautionary balances decreases as more precautionary balances are held.

5. If tastes cause large and frequent changes in the demand for money then the monetarist approach is more useful.

6. In general we think that an increase in the price of a substitute good should increase the demand for a good.

7. A credit card is a complement to money.

8. Changes in payments habits change money demand through the taste variable.

9. Velocity appears to be more stable, especially in the 1980s, if it is defined as the ratio of nominal income to the money stock that existed two quarters earlier.

10. It is not possible to predict velocity without a good prediction for money demand.

Self-Test: Multiple Choice

1. When an economist says someone has an excess supply of money, he or she
   a. is making a joke—no one has more money than they want.
   b. means that the person would rather have some good, service, or asset than the excess money he or she currently holds.
   c. means the person is holding money for a possible need that probably will not arise.
   d. means the person is holding money in the hope interest rates will rise and bond prices fall.
   e. Either c or d.

2. Precautionary balances would rise if
   a. anticipated expenses rose.
   b. unemployment, and therefore uncertainty, increased.
   c. interest rates became more stable so that potential capital gains declined.
   d. people are holding a large volume of liquid assets like Treasury securities.
   e. bond interest rates rose.

3. The benefit of holding a precautionary balance is that it avoids the cost of
   a. cutting planned expenditures.
   b. forced liquidation of an asset.
   c. borrowing.
   d. defaulting on an obligation.
   e. The least cost combination of the above.

4. The size of the precautionary balance is optimal if for a net interest cost of 6 percent, and a borrowing cost of 18 percent, the probability that the last dollar of the precautionary balance will be used is
   a. 108 percent
   b. 1 percent
   c. 33.33 percent
   d. 12 percent
   e. 24 percent

5. If income increases
   a. the demand for money will increase.
   b. the supply of money will increase.
   c. the supply of money will decrease.
   d. interest rates will fall.
   e. income velocity will fall.

6. The dominant explanation for the large errors in the statistical money demand equations is that
   a. inflation created uncertainty and large fluctuations in precautionary demand.
   b. more people became adept at playing the bond market so that investor optimism and pessimism had a larger influence on money demand.
   c. more people were paid cash bonuses based on performance that altered payments patterns and increased uncertainty.
   d. the OPEC price increases forced people to economize on cash holdings to an unanticipated degree.
   e. the higher interest rates and lower data-processing costs led to rapid financial innovation.

7. Statistical money demand functions generally include
   a. prices of complements.
   b. prices of substitutes.
   c. tastes.
   d. the costs of investing.
   e. a short-term interest rate.

8. If it were possible to costlessly and instantaneously convert high-interest bonds to low-interest money, then the demand for money would be
   a. zero.
   b. equal to monthly income.
   c. higher the higher the bond rate of interest.
   d. lower the higher the bond rate of interest.
   e. equal to precautionary plus speculative demand, and transaction demand would be zero.

9. The transaction demand for money increases if
   a. people convert bonds to cash more frequently due to low conversion fees.
   b. the bond rate of interest increases.
   c. income increases.
   d. people expect bond interest rates will decline.
   e. reduction of health care benefits increases uncertainty.

10. If the bond rate of interest increases, then the transaction

    demand for money _____ while the precautionary demand

    for money _____.
    a. increases; increases.
    b. increases; decreases.
    c. increases; does not change.
    d. decreases; increases.
    e. decreases; decreases.

Topics for Discussion

1. Tax reform has created many uncertainties. We all anticipate major reallocations of resources as marginal tax rates fall and many exemptions are lost. No one is certain how the changes will affect themselves. Do you think this uncertainty will add one more episode to the "case of the missing money"? Do you think precautionary or transactions demands will be more heavily affected? What variables would you add to a statistical money demand function to try to capture the effects?

2. Keynesians sometimes argue that money demand reflects business expectations. If you anticipate low yields in business, hold more money. In this scenerio, the business fluctuation causes the change in money demand—not the other way around. Is the quantity theory a useful device if such reverse causation is common? Is the remarkably steady growth of velocity, at least well into the 1970s, consistent with the scenario?

3. Milton Friedman has long complained that the case of the missing money and similar episodes are not evidence of an unstable money demand. He believes the episodes simply demonstrate the inadequacy of the bad statistical money demand functions traditionally used by economists. Compare the standard demand theory to the components of a statistical money demand function. Do you agree with Friedman? Where does this leave the Fed? Do they have an alternative to relying on the bad(?) functions economists use for fit?

Exercise Questions*

1. In this exercise you will be led to construct the marginal benefit schedule associated with the transactions demand for money. The basic idea is that the more often you exchange interest-earning bonds for cash, the less wealth you will need to tie up in cash that pays no interest. However, you will have to balance this benefit against the added costs of making frequent exchanges.

   We can make the exercise far more general by allowing symbols to represent amounts rather than specifying amounts. Let m be both your monthly income and your monthly expenses. You are paid your annual income of $12m$ on January 1 of each year. You are not paid again until the next January. (This is unrealistic but convenient.) Bonds pay a monthly interest rate of i, while the investment cost of exchanging bonds and cash (either direction) is b. This investment cost represents both actual fees and the inconvenience associated with the exchange. The fee does not change with the amount exchanged. You may buy bonds at any time. However, your monthly expenses must be paid in cash the first of every month.

   a. Does it make sense to buy bonds after January 1? (Remember that your total holdings of cash and bonds must decline over the year as expenses are paid.)

   b. Should you sell bonds while you still have cash?

   c. Does it make sense to keep a couple of months' worth of cash on hand on January 1 to avoid having to sell bonds for a few months?

*A similar exercise is available on a PC-compatible microcomputer disk. The program is described in "A Micro-Computer Program that Simulates the Baumol-Tobin Transactions Demand for Money" forthcoming in the summer 1987 issue of the *Journal of Economic Education*. The disk is available for $3.00 from Steven Beckman (Department of Economics, Wichita State University, Wichita, Kansas 67208).

d. About the only way to decide the precise money holdings that are optimal is to compare carefully selected possible money holding patterns. Given the answers to *a* and *b* we know that we can ignore patterns that include bond purchases after January 1, and ignore patterns that allow bond sales when some cash remains. Apparently we must plan bond sales so that we have a cash inventory that is drawn down by each month's expenses and precisely meets cash needs for some time period. Therefore, bond purchases and sales will be in multiples of the monthly expense.

While it is far from obvious, it is true that these cash inventories should all have the same initial size and be used to cover expenses for the same number of months. Consider a pattern that divides the year into two 6-month periods. The initial cash inventory would have to be $6m$, leaving $6m$ to invest for 6 months in bonds. At the beginning of the seventh month, you would sell all $6m$ in bonds to meet expenses for the rest of the year. Interest earnings from this program would be

_____ (number of bonds held $\times$ number of months held $\times$ monthly interest rate). For simplicity, we ignore the fact that the interest earnings could be used to meet expenses.

e. Dividing the year into three periods of 4 months each requires initial cash holdings of $4m$ and allows an initial bond purchase of $8m$. Bond sales of $4m$, at the beginning of months 5 and 9, would be required. Interest earnings from this program would

be _____ (add the interest earnings from 8 months' worth of bonds held for 4 months to the interest earnings from 4 months' worth of bonds held for 4 months).

f. Dividing the year into four periods of 3 months each requires initial cash holdings of _____ and results in interest earnings of _____.

g. Dividing the year into six periods of 2 months each requires initial cash holdings of _____ and results in interest.earnings of _____.

h. Dividing the year into twelve periods of 1 month each requires initial cash holdings of _____ and results in interest earnings of _____.

2. Use your calculations above to recommend a cash holding pattern to a client with a monthly income of $3,000 given a monthly interest rate of 1 percent and a fee of $200. Do this by comparing marginal benefit to marginal cost. The marginal benefit is the added interest earnings from additional bond sales. The marginal cost is the added fee for the added bond sale.

Answers to Self-Tests

Completion

1. liquid
2. investing
3. precautionary
4. transactions
5. substitutes; complements
6. income; tastes
7. tastes
8. the price of a substitute
9. money's own price
10. wire transfers; the dividend price ratio

True–False

1. True	6. True
2. False	7. False
3. False	8. True
4. True	9. True
5. False	10. False

Multiple Choice

1. *b*	6. *e*
2. *b*	7. *e*
3. *e*	8. *a*
4. *c*	9. *c*
5. *a*	10. *e*

Answers to Exercise Questions

1*a*. No. If you do buy bonds after January 1, you could have purchased them earlier when you had more of your annual income remaining and earned interest for a longer time period.

b. No. Wait until your cash is exhausted. This will allow you to earn interest longer.

c. It may, depending on the benefits and costs. The higher the fee for selling bonds the more likely that holding a cash inventory will be advantageous.

d. $(6m)(6)(i) = 36im$.

e. $(4)(i)(8m + 4m)$ = holding period, 4 months, times the monthly interest rate, i, times the amount of bonds held, $(8m + 4m) = 48im$.

f. $3m$; $(3)(i)(9m + 6m + 3m) = 54im$.

g. $2m$; $(2)(i)(10m + 8m + 6m + 4m + 2m) = 60im$.

h. $1m$; $(1)(i)(11m + 10m + 9m + 8m + 7m + 6m + 5m + 4m + 3m + 2m + 1m) = 66im$.

2. Your client should divide the year into three periods of 4 months each. The marginal benefit of the third period is $48im - 36im = 12im = 12(.01)(\$3,000) = \$360$. This is larger than the marginal cost of $200. However, if the client were to try four periods of 3 months each, the marginal benefit would be $54im - 48im = 6im = 6(.01)(\$3,000) = \$180$. So the fourth period's marginal revenue is less than its marginal cost.

CHAPTER 15 A Complete Keynesian Model

Learning Objectives

After studying this chapter, you should be able to

1. tell why a reduction in interest rates leads to a higher level of income, but an increase in income leads to a higher interest rate (by understanding the IS-LM diagram you should be able to explain and resolve this apparent contradiction).

2. use the IS-LM model to illustrate the effects of changing consumption, investment, taxes, government spending, money supply, and money demand on interest rates and income.

3. explain how an increase in government spending can crowd out private investment through higher interest rates, and crowd out production by reducing net exports.

4. explain how bond-financed government spending could shift the LM curve (this could accentuate or reduce the crowding-out effect).

Key Terms, Concepts, and Institutions

You should be able to define or explain

money market
simultaneous equilibrium
LM curve
expenditure slope
interest inelastic

crowding in
goods market
IS curve
crowding out
portfolio crowding out

Self-Test: Completion

1. The collection of interest income pairs where the demand and supply of goods and services are equal is called the _____.

2. The collection of interest income pairs where the demand and supply of money are equal is called the _____.

3. The LM curve is steep if money demand is more responsive to changes in _____ than _____.

4. The effect of a change in the interest rate on $C + I + G + X$ is called _____.

5. In this chapter the _____ refers to the total cost and difficulty of borrowing.

6. While the interest rate probably affects all the components of income, $C + I + G + X$, the effect on _____ is least certain.

7. The LM curve is not a supply curve or a demand curve but a _____ curve.

8. An interest income pair below both the IS and LM curves indicates excess _____ (supply or demand) in the money market and excess _____ (supply or demand) in the goods market.

9. As the supply of securities increases—and their price declines—the demand for money will rise if money and securities are _____.

10. Crowding in could occur either because money and securities are _____ or through the _____.

Self-Test: True–False

1. At an interest income pair above the IS curve, demand is less than production, unplanned inventories are accumulating, and businesses will cut back output.

2. At an interest income pair above the LM curve, money demand is greater than money supply and people will sell bonds in an attempt to acquire the money they want, forcing the interest rate higher.

3. If near-monies develop, the LM curve would shift toward lower interest rates and higher income.

4. If interest rates increase, investments increase because investments earn more.

5. Changes in money supply or money demand shift the LM curve, while changes in $C + I + G + X$ shift the IS curve as long as the changes are not caused by a change in bond interest rates or income. (Such changes are reflected in the slopes of the curves.)

6. Higher interest rates reduce investment. Therefore, whenever interest rates rise the IS curve shifts toward lower income.

7. Higher income increases the demand for money. Therefore, whenever income rises the LM curve shifts toward higher interest rates.

8. An increase in consumer confidence increases spending and therefore shifts the IS curve toward higher income.

9. Paying interest on checkable deposits increases the demand for money but since the change is induced by interest rates LM does not shift. (Remember that this happened in 1980.)

10. If the Fed kept the interest rate constant as G increased, then according to the IS-LM model income would rise by G times the multiplier.

Self-Test: Multiple Choice

1. If money demand were to increase, interest rates would tend to

   _____. This can be represented by shifting the LM curve

   _____.
   a. fall; up
   b. fall; down
   c. rise; up
   d. rise; down

2. If the LM curve shifts up, the change in interest rates causes investment to _____ and output to _____.
   a. rise; rise
   b. rise; fall
   c. fall; rise
   d. fall; fall

3. An increase in taxes shifts the _____.
   a. IS curve up.
   b. IS curve down.
   c. LM curve up.
   d. LM curve down.

4. A tax increase leads to a _____ interest rate and _____ income.
   a. lower; lower
   b. lower; higher
   c. higher; lower
   d. higher; higher

5. Assume investors suddenly become nervous about the future and reduce investment at every interest rate. This would shift the

   _____.
   a. IS curve up.
   b. IS curve down.
   c. LM curve up.
   d. LM curve down.

6. Continuing Question 5, the effect of investor panic is _____

   interest rates and _____ income.
   a. lower; lower
   b. lower; higher
   c. higher; lower
   d. higher; higher

7. The IS curve is downward sloping in part because
   a. higher prices reduce the demand for goods.
   b. higher income increases money demand and increases interest rates.
   c. lower interest rates stimulate investment and increase income.
   d. lower interest rates reduce profit, investment, and income.
   e. higher interest rates lead to a higher dollar value and increase our income.

8. The LM curve is upward sloping because
   a. higher prices increase money demand and interest rates.
   b. higher interest rates here increase foreigners' demand for the dollar so our income rises.
   c. higher interest rates increase the demand for money and income.
   d. lower interest rates stimulate investment and increase income.
   e. higher income increases money demand, which increases interest rates.

9. The IS curve is steep if expenditures are _____ to the interest rate and the multiplier is _____.
   a. sensitive; large
   b. sensitive; small
   c. insensitive; large
   d. insensitive; small

10. Portfolio crowding out results if
   a. people consider the future tax burden in current spending policies.
   b. people consider government bonds a money substitute so that an increase in bond wealth reduces money demand.
   c. people consider government bonds a money complement so that an increase in bond wealth increases money demand.
   d. higher interest rates increase the value of the dollar.
   e. people ignore the future tax burden in current spending policies.

Topics for Discussion

1. Before 1972, the value of the dollar did not vary directly with interest rates because of a treaty signed in 1944 that controlled exchange rates. By the mid-1970s the treaty was in a shambles. How do you think the emergence of a direct interest rate–exchange rate link affected the expenditure slope and crowding out?

2. Find some economic forecasts that discuss interest rates and income. Monday's outlook column of the *Wall Street Journal* will do nicely. Are the effects the *Journal* discusses included in the IS-LM model? Are the effects discussed in the article that are not part of the IS-LM model significant or insignificant?

3. Does the IS-LM model adequately discuss
   a. tax reform?
   b. oil price changes?
   c. changes in expected inflation?
   d. popular reaction to announced policies?
   e. changes in expected output?
   f. the time needed for changes to be apparent in income?

Exercise Questions

1. In this exercise you will construct and use an IS-LM diagram for an imaginary economy. In this economy the consumption function is $400 + .5Y$.

   a. What is the marginal propensity to consume?

   b. What is the multiplier?

   c. As the bond rate of interest rises the desired level of investment falls because the higher interest rate represents a higher borrowing cost. This is reflected in Table 15.1 below. Fill in the blanks of the table.

   Autonomous spending is desired investment plus the autonomous part of consumption, in this case 400. Recall that the multiplier times autonomous spending equals equilibrium income.

Table 15.1

Interest Rate	Desired Investment	Autonomous Spending	X the Multiplier =	Equilibrium Income
5%	600			
10%	400			
15%	200			

   These interest rate and income pairs are three points on this economy's IS curve. Plot these points on Figure 15.1.

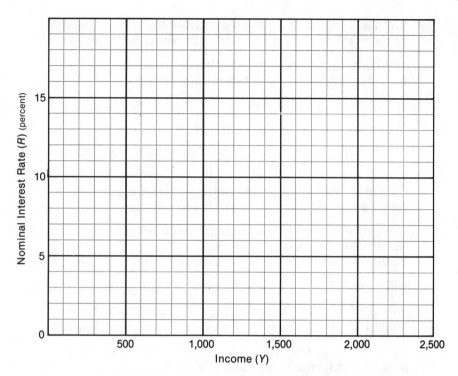

Figure 15.1 The Workers' IS-LM Diagram

2. The money-demand function for this economy is

$$M_d = .5Y - 40R.$$

Money supply is equal to $400. Find the income levels where the money supply equals money demand for the interest rates listed in Table 15.2.

Table 15.2 Equilibrium Points for the LM Curve

Nominal Interest Rate (R)	Income (Y)
15	$_____(a)
10	_____(b)
5	_____(c)

The numbers in Table 15.2 are points on the LM curve. Plot them on Figure 15.1. The workers' committee has two ways it could achieve full employment. It could form a government to increase production or it could increase the money stock. We can now calculate how much of each would be required. Full employment occurs at an income level of (*d:* _____). To maintain this output level the workers committee must invest (*e:* _____) which they will not do unless the interest rate is (*f:* _____). At this interest and income combination the money demand is (*g:* _____). To reach this level the money stock must be raised by (*h:* _____). On Figure 15.1, draw the LM curve for this money stock and label it LM' (you just found one point and LM' is parallel to LM through this point).

3. Alternatively, the workers' committee could sell bonds and use the proceeds to finance public works. At an income level of $2,000 and a money supply of $400 we know the interest rate will be (*a:* _____) and the workers' committee will invest only (*b:* _____). Based on the formula that appears in Table 15.1, we need (400 + 200 + G)(2) = $2,000. G needs to be (*c:* _____). On Figure 15.1, draw the IS curve for this government spending level and label it IS' (you have just calculated one point and IS' is parallel to IS through this point).

Answers to Self-Tests

Completion

1. IS curve
2. LM curve
3. income; interest rate
4. the expenditure slope
5. interest rate
6. government spending
7. market equilibrium
8. demand; demand
9. complements
10. substitutes; accelerator

True–False

1. True	6. False
2. False	7. False
3. True	8. True
4. False	9. False
5. True	10. True

Multiple Choice

1. *c*	6. *a*
2. *d*	7. *c*
3. *b*	8. *e*
4. *a*	9. *d*
5. *b*	10. *c*

Answers to Exercise Questions

1*a*. .5
 b. 2
 c.

Table 15.1

Interest Rate	Desired Investment	Autonomous Spending	× the Multiplier =	Equilibrium Income
5%	600	1,000	2	2,000
10%	400	800	2	1,600
15%	200	600	2	1,200

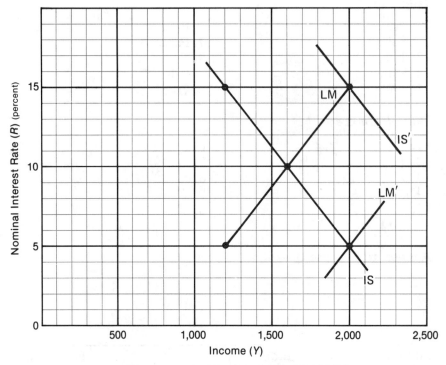

Answer to Figure 15.1 The Worker's IS-LM Diagram

2a. 2,000   e. 600
 b. 1,600   f. 5 percent
 c. 1,200   g. $800
 d. 2,000   h. $400

3a. 15 percent
 b. 200
 c. $400

CHAPTER 16   The Monetarist Approach

Learning Objectives

After studying this chapter, you should be able to

1. state the basic principles of the quantity theory.

2. describe the Chicago approach, and how Milton Friedman's theory is different from the quantity theory.

3. state the Keynesian criticisms of the quantity theory and Friedman's adaptation of the quantity theory.

4. describe the monetarist transmission process for changes in the money stock.

5. describe Andersen and Jordan's St. Louis approach, and the empirical results obtained with this model.

6. know the six major issues in the Keynesian-monetarist dispute.

7. state the assumptions and results from Patinkin's real balance approach.

8. describe the Brunner-Meltzer model and the implications of empirical results obtained from this model.

Key Terms, Concepts, and Institutions

You should be able to define or explain

St. Louis approach   money illusion
high-employment variables   real effects
Brunner-Meltzer analysis   inside money
stock effect   quantity theory of money

disequilibrium in the govern-   Chicago approach
   ment sector   "black box"
real balance approach   outside money

Self-Test: Completion

1. If the data show little correlation between the deficit and
changes in nominal income, the _____ theory is suspect.

2. Brunner and Meltzer view government bonds and capital as
(substitutes/complements).

3. You suffer from _____ if you react to nominal, as opposed
to real, variables.

4. Andersen and Jordan are associated with the _____ model.

5. Money which represents a claim against someone in the private
sector is called _____ money.

6. According to _____, the economy cannot come to
equilibrium unless the budget is balanced.

7. According to the St. Louis approach, _____ policy has
strong, lasting effects, but the net effect of _____ policy is
zero.

8. The real balance approach was developed by _____.

9. For the quantity theory to be valid, causation must run from
_____ to _____, and not vice versa.

10. All three monetarist models spring from the _____ theory.

Self-Test: True–False

1. According to Milton Friedman, the value of k, the proportion
of nominal income that people want to hold as money, is a stable
number.

2. The work of Ando and Modigliani supports the conclusions of
the St. Louis approach.

3. According to Patinkin's real balance approach, monetary variables do not affect real variables in the long run, given completely flexible wages and prices, no money illusion, no redistribution

effects, a balanced budget, no government bonds outstanding, and currency as the only type of money.

4. According to Brunner and Meltzer, if the government issues money to pay for a deficit, prices and nominal income rise permanently.

5. Andersen and Jordan use actual government receipts and deficits to help explain changes in income.

6. A criticism of the Brunner-Meltzer analysis is that it ignores the changes in the stocks of assets.

7. According to the real balance approach, money is a veil which affects real variables.

8. In principle, the Brunner-Meltzer approach could produce the Keynesian conclusion that fiscal policy has a powerful effect on income.

9. Brunner and Meltzer assert that aggregate demand will continue to increase as long as there is a deficit.

10. If there are government bonds and inside money, the real balance approach asserts that prices and money will not change proportionately.

Self-Test: Multiple Choice

1. According to Brunner and Meltzer, an increase in aggregate demand will reduce the deficit for all of the following reasons *except*
   a. the resulting increase in wealth increases the proportion of income consumed.
   b. the rise in investment and consumption expenditures increases nominal income and, hence, tax receipts.
   c. as nominal income increases, people move into higher tax brackets.
   d. rising prices lower the real value of interest payments on the government's debt.
   e. All of the above are reasons why an increase in aggregate demand reduces the deficit.

2. Patinkin assumes all of the following *except*
   a. flexible wages and prices.
   b. money and bonds are complements.
   c. people do not suffer from money illusion.

d. there are no redistribution effects from changes in prices.

e. taxpayers are indifferent to the real value of the government's debt.

3. According to Patinkin's real balance approach, if there are no government bonds outstanding and currency is the only money, a rise in the nominal money stock will

a. increase the rate of interest.

b. increase real income.

c. increase prices proportionately.

d. increase prices less than proportionately.

e. increase the yield on capital.

4. The Andersen and Jordan technique

a. stresses the stock of assets and the relative prices of assets.

b. asserts that monetary variables do not affect real variables.

c. is a single-equation technique.

d. is a large-scale econometric model.

e. specifies the transmission mechanism by which monetary policy affects income.

5. Which of the following economists performed a study which somewhat discredits the St. Louis approach?

a. Milton Friedman

b. David Meiselman

c. Michael Keran

d. Franco Modigliani

e. Leonall Andersen

6. The work of Brunner and Meltzer

a. takes no account of disequilibrium in the government sector.

b. develops an explicit transmission mechanism.

c. concludes that fiscal policy is the dominant impulse that drives nominal income.

d. stresses the stock of assets and changes in the prices of assets.

e. b and d.

7. The St. Louis approach

a. found that monetary policy has no lasting effect on nominal income.

b. argues that changes in monetary variables cause changes in nominal income.

c. does not explain how monetary variables affect income.

d. considers the interest rate to be an exogenous variable.

e. is a formalized model of the quantity theory that brings out its assumptions.

8. According to the Brunner-Meltzer approach, if government spending increases and the government issues money to finance it,
    a. output will temporarily increase.
    b. the price of money in dollar terms falls.
    c. the price of money in dollar terms rises.
    d. the prices of all other items fall.
    e. prices and real income rise permanently.

9. According to the real balance approach,
    a. creditors experience an increase in real wealth if prices rise.
    b. a uniform change in prices does not affect the value of government debt.
    c. the interest rate depends on real income.
    d. a uniform change in prices does not affect the real value of physical assets.
    e. the demand for labor depends on nominal wages.

10. The real balance approach specifies that
    a. under certain conditions, changes in the money stock bring about a strictly proportional change in the price level.
    b. people do not suffer from money illusion.
    c. equilibrium will always occur at full employment if wages and prices are completely flexible.
    d. the existence of government bonds outstanding and inside money implies that money and prices need not change proportionately.
    e. All of the above.

Topics for Discussion

1. Compare and contrast the three major variants of monetarism.

2. What are the policy implications for each of the three approaches?

3. Describe the ways in which the Brunner-Meltzer approach differs from the Keynesian approach.

4. Is the St. Louis approach consistent with the Brunner-Meltzer approach? Why or why not?

5. How could a change in income affect the money stock? Is this inconsistent with the St. Louis approach?

Exercise Questions

1. According to the Brunner-Meltzer approach

   a. if the supply of government bonds decreases, the demand for capital (increases/decreases). Investment and income (increase/decrease). Fiscal policy (can/cannot) affect income.

   b. if the government runs a surplus and retires some of its bonds, wealth (increases/decreases), causing investment and consumption to (increase/decrease). Aggregate demand (increases/decreases) and income (rises/falls), causing tax receipts to (rise/fall). The surplus will (narrow/widen).

2. Benjamin M. Friedman, using updated estimates of the St. Louis equation, found a significant government spending multiplier of about 1.5, as well as a relatively strong impact for monetary policy. What are the implications of these findings? What are the implications given that a later study of the St. Louis people, done in percentage terms, yields the familiar St. Louis result?

Answers to Self-Tests

Completion

1. Keynesian
2. complements
3. money illusion
4. St. Louis
5. inside
6. Brunner and Meltzer
7. monetary; fiscal
8. Don Patinkin
9. monetary variables; income
10. quantity

True–False

1. False	6. False
2. False	7. False
3. True	8. True
4. True	9. True
5. False	10. True

Multiple Choice

1. *a*	6. *e*
2. *b*	7. *b*
3. *c*	8. *a*
4. *c*	9. *d*
5. *d*	10. *e*

Answers to Exercise Questions

1*a*. decreases; decrease; can

  b. decreases; decrease; decreases; falls; fall; narrow

2. These findings are consistent with Keynesian thinking. The title of Friedman's article was "Even the St. Louis Model Now Believes in Fiscal Policy," in the *Journal of Money, Credit, and Banking* (May 1977): 365–67. The later study suggests that Friedman's results are sensitive to changes in the units of measurement and casts doubt on his findings.

CHAPTER 17　The Monetarist-Keynesian Debate in Perspective

Learning Objectives

After studying this chapter, you should be able to

1. list the points of agreement and disagreement between Keynesian and monetarist propositions.

2. explain the policy implications of these propositions.

3. show how the interest elasticity of expenditure relates to the "only money matters" position.

Key Terms, Concepts, and Institutions

You should be able to define or explain

asset-stock approach
expenditures-flow approach
NAIRU (nonaccelerating inflation rate of unemployment)

Self-Test: Completion

1. According to the _____, money has direct effects through wealth on income, prices, and employment.

2. Keynesians believe monetary policy could be ineffective if the demand for investment is (elastic/inelastic) with respect to the rate of interest.

3. According to the monetarists, money exerts its influence through _____ and _____.

4. _____ assert that government debt is wealth.

5. _____ believe that the unemployment-inflation trade-off exists long enough to be useful.

6. A famous economist once said, "In the long run we are all dead." The speaker was probably a _____.

7. Monetarists and Keynesians agree that, given current institutional realities, there is a practical lower limit to the rate of unemployment called the _____.

8. Monetarists believe in _____ equation models.

9. Monetarists believe that the government (should/should not) engage in short-run stabilization policies.

10. Keynesians (do/do not) believe that the slopes of the IS and LM curves determine the effectiveness of monetary policy.

Self-Test: True–False

1. Monetarists are concerned mainly with expounding causal relationships.

2. Keynesians believe the unemployment rate can remain above the NAIRU for long periods of time.

3. Monetarists believe the rate of unemployment is independent of the rate of inflation.

4. Monetarists believe that monetary policy should be used to stabilize the economy.

5. Monetarists emphasize the effects of expectations more than Keynesians do.

6. Monetarists have great faith in the abilities of government economic forecasters.

7. Keynesians believe a lower rate of inflation would require substantial unemployment.

8. Monetarists agree that an inelastic demand for investment would imply that monetary policy is ineffective.

9. Keynesians believe that monetary policy is totally ineffective.

10. Keynesians and monetarists agree that it is not possible for any policy to long sustain a rate of unemployment below NAIRU.

Extra Help: A Comparison of Keynesian and Monetarist Positions[1]

Keynesian Propositions	Monetarist Propositions
1. The money stock can affect income, but so can other variables. Money is no more or less important than any other variable.	1. Money is the dominant force driving income.
2. The private economy is inherently unstable.	2. The private economy is inherently stable.
3. Monetary policy works indirectly by affecting interest rates.	3. Monetary policy works directly through wealth effects and by changing the relative prices of assets.
4. The appropriate horizon is the short run.	4. The appropriate horizon is the long run.
5. An elastic demand for money or an inelastic demand for investment may make monetary policy ineffective.	5. Liquidity traps are unlikely and an inelastic demand for investment does not preclude effective monetary policy.
6. Bonds are good substitutes for money, so that an increase in the supply of bonds raises the prices of real assets, enhancing the effect of deficit financing.	6. Bonds are good substitutes for capital, blunting the expansionary effects of deficit financing.
7. Government debt is wealth.	7. Government debt is not wealth.
8. Forecasting is accurate enough to permit policy actions to make the economy more stable, and policymakers can use these forecasts efficiently.	8. Government policy should not be used to stabilize the economy in the short run, as it is the major source of destabilization. The money supply should be increased at a constant rate.
9. The slopes of the IS and LM curves determine the effectiveness of monetary policy.	9. The slopes of the IS and LM curves do not determine the effectiveness of monetary policy.
10. Monetary and fiscal policy may be used to stabilize the economy, but fiscal policy is more effective and operates with a shorter lag. Money has its main influence when created to finance fiscal policy.	10. Monetary policy is more effective than fiscal policy. Fiscal policy has effects only to the extent that monetary policy is accommodating.
11. The rate of inflation is inversely related to the unemployment rate. The unemployment rate can therefore be reduced by incurring the appropriate rate of inflation.	11. There is a natural rate of unemployment (NAIRU) which will evolve at any constant rate of inflation. There is no long-run trade-off between unemployment and inflation.

[1]This list is adapted from Terry L. Rush, "Some Theoretical Aspects of the Keynesian Monetarist Debate," *Revista Internationale* (March 1976): 235–36.

Keynesian Propositions	*Monetarist Propositions*
12. The economy can come to equilibrium below full employment.	12. Prices and wages are more flexible than Keynesian theory suggests. The economy naturally tends to full-employment equilibrium.
13. Single equation models are too simple.	13. The appropriate model is a single-equation model.

Points of Agreement

1. The demand for money is elastic to interest rates, but the short run elasticity is low. Monetary policy can have effects.

2. Interest elasticities of consumption and investment do not entirely justify either extreme.

3. There is a natural rate of unemployment (NAIRU). No policy can sustain an unemployment rate below NAIRU for long.

Self-Test: Multiple Choice

1. According to (Keynesian/monetarist) theory, the economy is inherently (stable/unstable).
   a. Keynesian; stable
   b. Keynesian; unstable
   c. monetarist; stable
   d. monetarist; unstable
   e, b and c.

2. If bonds are good substitutes for capital, an increase in the supply of bonds for the purpose of financing the deficit
   a. will cause crowding out to occur.
   b. will cause the demand for capital to increase.
   c. will enhance the effect of government spending.
   d. will raise the prices of real assets.
   e. b, c, and d.

3. All of the following are monetarist propositions *except:*
   a. Bonds are good substitutes for capital.
   b. Money exerts its influence only by affecting the rate of interest.
   c. Government debt is not wealth.

d. The money supply should be increased at a constant rate of growth.

e. All of the above are monetarist propositions.

4. All of the following are Keynesian propositions *except:*

a. Monetary and fiscal policy are appropriate tools for the short-run stabilization of the economy.

b. The rate of inflation is inversely related to the rate of unemployment.

c. The appropriate horizon is the short run.

d. An inelastic (with respect to the interest rate) demand for money reduces the effectiveness of monetary policy.

e. All of the above are Keynesian propositions.

5. Which of the following economists is a Keynesian?

a. Milton Friedman

b. Leonall Anderson

c. James Tobin

d. David Meiselman

e. Karl Brunner

Topics for Discussion

1. Discuss some ways in which the monetarists and Keynesians differ in respect to the transmissions mechanism for monetary variables.

2. Which political party is likely to be most sympathetic to Keynesian doctrine? To monetarist doctrine?

Exercise Questions

1. "In one respect, the [Federal Reserve] System has remained completely consistent . . . in blaming all problems on external influences beyond its control and taking credit for any and all favorable occurrences. It thereby continues to promote the myth that the private economy is unstable, while its behavior continues to document the reality that government is today the major source of economic instability."

Is the author a Keynesian or a monetarist?

2. ". . . liquidity preference may become virtually absolute in the sense that everyone prefers cash to holding a debt which yields so low a rate of interest. . . ."

Is the author a Keynesian or monetarist?

Answers to Self-Tests

Completion

1. Monetarists
2. inelastic
3. wealth effects; by changing the relative prices of assets
4. Keynesians
5. Keynesians
6. Keynesian (as a matter of fact, it was Keynes)
7. NAIRU (nonaccelerating inflation rate of unemployment)
8. single
9. should not
10. do

True–False

1. False	6. False
2. True	7. True
3. True	8. False
4. False	9. False
5. True	10. True

Multiple Choice

1. *e*	4. *d*
2. *a*	5. *c*
3. *b*	

Answers to Exercise Questions

1. The authors are monetarist: Milton Friedman in Milton and Rose Friedman, "The Anatomy of a Crisis," *Journal of Portfolio Management* (Fall 1979), p. 21.

2. The author is Keynesian: John Maynard Keynes in *The General Theory of Employment, Interest, and Money*. New York: Harcourt, Brace and World, Inc., 1936, p. 207.

CHAPTER 18   Inflation and Unemployment

Learning Objectives

After studying this chapter, you should be able to

1. state the implications of the Phillips curve and the expectations-augumented Phillips curve.

2. explain the concept of the NAIRU.

3. explain the slopes of the aggregate demand and aggregate supply curves.

4. give examples of demand- and supply-side shocks, and explain why these shocks are not likely to cause persistent inflation.

5. state the advantages and disadvantages of the various policies to fight inflation.

6. cite causes of unemployment.

7. explain the "new classical" theory.

8. explain why a major inflation requires an increase in the money stock.

Key Terms, Concepts, and Institutions

You should be able to define or explain

inflation

creeping inflation

hyperinflation

consumer price index

unemployment

frictional unemployment

natural rate of unemployment
  (NAIRU)

aggregate demand

aggregate supply

supply-side shocks

demand-side shocks

short-run Phillips curve   income policy
expectations-augumented   "jawboning"
  Phillips curve   "social contract"
new classical theory   indexing

Self-Test: Completion

1. _____ unemployment is needed for an efficient economy.

2. The rate of inflation associated with any given output level will

   be _____ as productivity declines.

3. The _____ becomes a vertical line at the NAIRU when people correctly anticipate the inflation rate.

4. The unemployment rate that is just high enough to avoid ever-

   accelerating inflation is called the _____.

5. Moderate inflation, perhaps 3 or 5 percent per year, is called

   _____ inflation.

6. Elimination of minimum wage laws and programs to retrain the

   unemployed might _____ the NAIRU.

7. Stabilization policies tend to _____ the effects of anti-inflation measures.

8. The Phillips curve relates the rate of _____ to the rate of

   _____.

9. _____ economists believe that fluctuations in output and employment are primarily due to a temporary confusion of relative and absolute prices.

10. Pervasive crop failures would be an example of a _____-side shock.

Self-Test: True–False

1. The aggregate demand curve slopes downward because as the price level rises, real wealth and incomes fall, so that people reduce their purchases and output falls.

2. An increase in the demand for money will cause the aggregate demand curve to shift upward.

3. The most likely cause for a major inflation is an increase in the money stock.

4. Other things being equal, wages increase faster when unemployment is low.

5. No steady rate of inflation is possible if the unemployment rate is below NAIRU.

6. A rise in unemployment may be due to an increase in the marginal efficiency of investment.

7. A one-time rise in the interest rate increases aggregate demand and may account for prolonged inflation.

8. Most economists believe that wages and prices are much more flexible than the "new classicals" believe.

9. An increase in aggregate demand initially causes output and prices to rise.

10. The short-run Phillips curve suggests a positive relationship between inflation and unemployment.

Self-Test: Multiple Choice

1. Changes in price are related _____ to changes in productivity and _____ to changes in wages.
   a. negatively; negatively
   b. negatively; positively
   c. positively; positively
   d. positively; negatively
   e. directly; inversely

2. Which of the following might cause a *decrease* in aggregate demand?
   a. an increase in government spending
   b. a reduction in taxes
   c. a reduction in the money supply
   d. an increase in the money supply
   e. *a, b,* and *d.*

3. Other things being equal, an increase in aggregate demand will
   a. reduce employment.
   b. reduce output.
   c. lower prices.
   d. raise prices.
   e. increase the real money supply.

4. All of the following are examples of supply-side shocks *except*
   a. a decrease in the marginal propensity to consume.
   b. rising labor costs.
   c. an increase in import prices.
   d. an increase in taxes.
   e. *a* and *d*.
   f. *b* and *c*.

5. A decrease in aggregate supply
   a. lowers prices.
   b. raises employment.
   c. decreases employment.
   d. increases the real money supply.
   e. increases output.

6. All of the following are supply-side shocks which contributed to high inflation in the 1970s *except*
   a. the actions of OPEC through its embargo on oil supplies in 1973 and the quadrupling of imported oil prices in 1973–74.
   b. crop failures around the world at a time when carryover stocks of grain were low.
   c. the large tax cut in 1975.
   d. the drop in Iranian oil production.
   e. the rising costs of home ownership.

7. NAIRU rose substantially in the 1970s for all of the following reasons *except*
   a. more women entering the labor force.
   b. the tendency of teenagers to change jobs frequently.
   c. the entrance of teenage baby boomers into the job market.
   d. a decrease in racial discrimination.
   e. All of the above are factors which account for the increase in NAIRU in the 1970s.

8. Which of the following would increase prices?
   a. a decrease in the marginal efficiency of investment
   b. an increase in the money stock
   c. a decrease in import prices
   d. an increase in aggregate supply
   e. None of the above.

Topics for Discussion

1. The *Wall Street Journal* reported on August 23, 1983, that "a drought that some say is the worst since the dust bowl harvest of 1937 continues to propel grain and soybean prices higher. But

the price surge also reflects a wave of crop-buying by foreign interests, including the Soviet Union and the seemingly anxious Japanese." Discuss the effects of these developments on aggregate demand, the price level, and the level of unemployment.

2. The *Wall Street Journal* reported on October 2, 1986, that "a longshoremen's strike shut ports from Main to Virginia, catching shippers by surprise and threatening long-term damage to the Northeast ports." Discuss the effects of this action on aggregate demand, aggregate supply, the price level, and output.

Exercise Questions

1. Suppose the administration embarks on a campaign to lower inflation by decreasing government spending and decreasing the money supply. On Figure 18.1, show how these policies will affect aggregate demand and/or long-run aggregate supply.

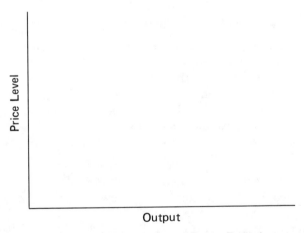

Figure 18.1 Aggregate Demand and Long-Run Aggregate Supply

2. How do each of the following increase the level of inflation?

   a. tariffs, quotas, and voluntary restraints, such as the efforts to restrain Japanese auto imports

   b. the value of the dollar falls on the foreign exchange market

c. drought in the Midwest

d. factories operating at rates higher than their optimal capacity

e. increasing demands by unions as unemployment decreases

Answers to Self-Tests

Completion

1. frictional
2. higher
3. Expectations-augmented Phillips curve
4. NAIRU or natural rate of unemployment
5. creeping
6. lower
7. weaken
8. wage (price) increases; unemployment
9. New classical
10. supply

True–False

1. True	6. False
2. True	7. False
3. True	8. False
4. True	9. True
5. True	10. False

Multiple Choice

1. *b*	5. *c*
2. *c*	6. *c*
3. *d*	7. *d*
4. *e*	8. *b*

Answers to Exercise Questions

1.

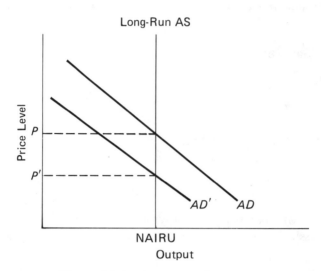

Answer to Figure 18.1 Aggregate Demand and Long-Run
Aggregate Supply

Decreasing government spending and decreasing the money
supply decrease aggregate demand and do not change NAIRU,
lowering the level of prices with no change in output in the
long run.

2a. Supply is curtailed and prices rise, not only for imported goods
but for competing goods as well.

b. The prices of imported goods will rise.

c. The supply of basic grains, etc., is reduced, raising prices.

d. After this point, productivity tends to decline because factories
are using marginal equipment, overtime shifts, and other more
costly production methods. A decrease in productivity increases
prices.

e. An increase in wages without a corresponding increase in production increases prices.

CHAPTER 19   The Goals of Monetary Policy

Learning Objectives

After studying this chapter, you should be able to

1. discuss the conflicts among the Fed's goals.

2. explain why zero unemployment is impractical and undesirable.

3. compare the costs of unemployment and inflation.

4. show why the coordination of monetary and fiscal policy can eliminate some of the conflicts but not all.

5. explain why interest-rate stabilization can force the Fed to monetize the government debt.

Key Terms, Concepts, and Institutions

You should be able to define or explain

employment level
price stability
anticipated inflation
unanticipated inflation
redistribution of income
after-tax return
economic growth

interest-rate stability
financial stability
allocative burden of a restrictive
  policy
conflicts among goals
coordination of policy
government budget constraint

Self-Test: Completion

1. The single most important conflict between the goals of the Fed is between high employment and _____ stability.

2. The costs of _____ inflation are higher than the costs of _____ inflation.

3. We could achieve both high employment and a low rate of interest by a combination of expansive _____ policy and contractionary _____ policy.

4. Unemployment that results from new entrants in the labor force, occupational mismatch, or job search activities is called _____ unemployment.

5. Inflation can result in a negative after-tax interest income because _____ interest is taxed.

6. If the inflation rate is 15 percent, the interest rate is 20 percent, and the tax rate is 50 percent, then the real after-tax return is _____ percent.

7. President Carter voiced the concern that trust in government and social institutions is eroded by _____.

8. Fluctuating interest rates can redistribute wealth since higher interest rates imply everyone's bond holdings are worth _____.

9. Both fiscal and monetary policy shift aggregate _____, and therefore both face the short-run trade-off between _____ and _____.

10. If Congress passed a law that adjusted all tax brackets and exemptions by 10 percent whenever prices rose 10 percent then we could say the tax system was _____ for inflation.

Self-Test: True–False

1. The frictional level of unemployment is known.

2. The number of people unemployed depends on the level and duration of unemployment-compensation benefits.

3. The optimal level of unemployment is no unemployment.

4. Inflation increases the taxes that corporations pay since depreciation is taxed on a replacement-cost basis.

5. The fact that inflation pushes people into higher tax brackets may lead to a larger government.

6. Since inflation increases the value of real property, inflation increases the value of stock prices.

7. Inflation increases the real value of savings.

8. Inflation hurts debtors and helps creditors.

9. Inflation reduces our ability to plan for the future.

10. The Fed could increase investment and growth by reducing inflation and its associated uncertainty.

11. It is widely believed that the Fed eased policy in the summer of 1982 to avoid widespread bankruptcies in what was a fragile financial system.

12. The goals of stable exchange rates and stable interest rates are in fundamental conflict.

13. The financial planning of firms is aided by stable interest rates.

14. Interest-rate stability and price stability conflict in the long run.

15. The problem of conflict among goals arises because the Fed does not have as many independent tools as it has targets and constraints.

Self-Test: Multiple Choice

1. The following is a cost of *anticipated* inflation:
   a. Prices will be out of equilibrium for short periods between price changes.
   b. Taxes are redistributed.
   c. Income is redistributed.
   d. Uncertainty reduces growth.
   e. All of the above.

2. Unemployment figures tend to be understated because
   a. some people quit looking for work out of discouragement.
   b. two members of a household may both be looking for a single job (they may not care which one works).
   c. some look for work just to be able to collect benefits.
   d. part-time workers are considered to be unemployed.
   e. All the above lead to unemployment figures that overstate unemployment.

3. It is difficult to decide if unemployment is too high or too low because
   a. while we can accurately measure unemployment, we do not know the optimal level of unemployment.
   b. we cannot accurately measure unemployment and we do not know the optimal level of unemployment.
   c. while we know the optimal level of unemployment, we cannot accurately measure unemployment.
   d. the level of unemployment needed for price stability (about 4 percent) is below the frictional level of unemployment (about 6 percent).
   e. the unemployment data are gathered only once every year.

4. In recent years, inflation has
   a. helped the poor.
   b. redistributed income within income classes.
   c. led to high nominal interest rates.
   d. Only b and c.
   e. a, b, and c.

5. We could stimulate economic growth through a low real interest rate if
   a. the Fed would allow rapid money growth.
   b. both monetary and fiscal policy were tight.
   c. both monetary and fiscal policy were loose.
   d. there was a budget surplus and expansionary monetary policy.
   e. the government reduced its expenditures on research and development.

6. A reduction in interest rates hurts
   a. bondholders.
   b. those who borrow long term and lend short term.
   c. savings and loans.
   d. corporations about to sell bonds.
   e. people with large holdings of commercial paper.

7. The goals of economic growth and price stability
   a. conflict in the long run and in the short run.
   b. conflict in the long run because price stability increases interest rates.
   c. conflict only in the short run since price stability may require short-run recessions.
   d. never conflict.
   e. are relatively minor goals.

8. The goals of interest-rate stability and price stability
   a. conflict in both the long and short run.
   b. conflict in the short run only.
   c. conflict in the long run only.
   d. never conflict.

9. The authors suggest that if the Fed had to pick just one goal to follow that one goal should be
   a. interest-rate stability.
   b. financial stability.
   c. economic growth.
   d. high employment.
   e. stable prices.

10. The authors suggest a price-stability goal would lead the Fed into error if
    a. oil prices rose during a period of high unemployment.
    b. the government went on a spending spree.
    c. rapid rates of investment led to low levels of unemployment.
    d. institutional changes led to a low money demand and low interest rates.
    e. there is deflation and high unemployment.

11. The Fed faces a dilemma if it wants to stabilize interest rates in the short run and keep prices stable if
    a. interest rates and prices are rising.
    b. interest rates are rising and prices are falling.
    c. interest rates and prices are falling.
    d. interest rates are falling and prices are rising.
    e. Both a and c.

12. Price stability and high employment come into conflict if
    a. there is deflation and unemployment.
    b. there is inflation and unemployment.
    c. there is inflation and overemployment.
    d. aggregate demand suddenly drops.
    e. Both a and c.

Topics for Discussion

1. Should the Fed explain which goal is being pursued at the expense of others?

2. What is the connection between the government's budget constraint and Fed policy?

3. If we need as many tools as we have goals in order to achieve all our goals, why can't we use fiscal policy to combat unemployment and monetary policy to combat inflation?

4. If you were in a position to mandate which goal(s) the Fed must pursue, which goal(s) would you choose? Defend your choice.

5. Why is price stability a poor goal if there is a major oil-price increase?

Exercise Questions

Use the IS-LM and aggregate demand/aggregate supply diagrams to illustrate the conflicts in Fed goals.

1. Assume the Fed wishes to maintain the current rate of interest but wants to reduce output in order to reduce inflation. The current economic situation is shown in Figure 19.1.

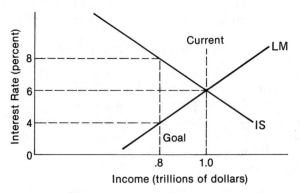

Figure 19.1 IS-LM Curves

To achieve the income goal the Fed could (*a:* increase/reduce) the money stock. This would shift the (*b:* IS/LM) curve (*c:* up/down). If government policy did not change, the interest rate would be (*d:* 4 percent/6 percent/8 percent). The government could help the Fed to achieve its goals by (*e:* increasing taxes and reducing government spending/reducing taxes and increasing government spending). This would shift the (*f:* IS/LM curve (*g:* up/down). The two policies (*h:* could/could not) be coordinated to achieve the interest rate and income goals.

Alternatively, if the government (*i:* increased/decreased) government spending to achieve the income goal and the Fed kept the money stock constant, the interest rate would be (*j:* 4 percent/6 percent/8 percent).

-158-

2. Assume the Fed wishes to increase employment without changing the price level. The current economic condition is shown in
Figure 19.2.

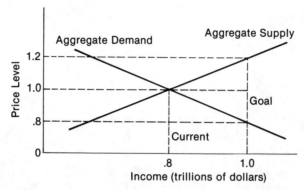

Figure 19.2   Aggregate Supply/Aggregate Demand Curves

If the Fed acts alone to achieve the income level of $1 trillion,
it will (*a:* increase/decrease) the money stock which will shift the
aggregate (*b:* demand/supply) curve (*c:* up/down). The new price
level would be (*d:* .8/1.0/1.2). The government (*e:* can/cannot)
help since changes in government spending and taxes affect
aggregate (*f:* supply/demand). To resolve this conflict, we need
to find some way to (*g:* increase/decrease) aggregate (*h:* supply/
demand). Reagan used to claim he had just such a tool in the
form of tax cuts. Do you remember the argument?

Answers to Self-Tests

Completion

1. price
2. unanticipated; anticipated
3. monetary; fiscal
4. frictional
5. nominal
6. −5
7. inflation
8. less
9. demand; inflation; unemployment
10. indexed

True–False

1. False
2. True
3. False
4. False
5. True
6. False
7. False
8. False

9. True
10. True
11. True
12. False
13. True
14. False
15. True

Multiple Choice

1. *a*
2. *a*
3. *b*
4. *e*
5. *d*
6. *b*

7. *c*
8. *b*
9. *e*
10. *a*
11. *e*
12. *b*

Answers to Exercise Questions

1*a*. reduce
 b. LM
 c. up
 d. 8 percent
 e. increasing taxes and reducing government spending
 f. IS
 g. down
 h. could
 i. decreased
 j. 4 percent

2*a*. increase
 b. demand
 c. up
 d. 1.2
 e. cannot
 f. demand
 g. increase
 h. supply

CHAPTER 20 Tools of Monetary Policy

Learning Objectives

After studying this chapter, you should be able to

1. state which Fed tools are general controls and which are selective controls.

2. describe each of the Fed's tools, how they work, and how the Fed would use them to pursue expansionary (or contractionary) monetary policy.

3. list the advantages and disadvantages of each of the Fed's tools.

4. distinguish between dynamic and defensive operations.

Key Terms, Concepts, and Institutions

You should be able to define or explain

general controls
selective controls
announcement effect
adjusted credit
extended credit
discounting
"make a market"
repos (repurchase agreements)
"feel of the market"

reverse repo (matched sales purchase)
dynamic operations
defensive operations
discounting
margin
moral suasion
open-market operations
discount rate
rediscounting

Self-Test: Completion

1. _____ are used when the Fed wishes to temporarily *absorb* reserves.

2. Government securities dealers are said to _____ in Treasury bills when they hold an inventory of them.

3. A repurchase agreement is an example of a _____ operation.

4. _____ credit is short-term credit, intended to tide depository institutions over until they can get other funds.

5. _____ tools affect the whole economy, while _____ tools affect particular sectors.

6. _____ credit is available when a depository institution experiences special difficulties, or when a broad group of depository institutions experiences liquidity strains.

7. The process of deducting the interest due from the face value of the borrower's promissory note is called _____.

8. The Fed has the power to set the _____, or down payment, required when purchasing stock.

9. _____ refers to written or oral appeals from the Fed.

10. An increase in the reserve-requirement ratio _____ the money multiplier.

Self-Test: True–False

1. The primary function of required reserves is to provide reserves in the event of an unexpected deposit outflow.

2. The Fed is authorized to deal only in U.S. government Treasury bills in its open-market operations.

3. The Fed uses repos to temporarily provide reserves.

4. Most of the Fed's open-market operations are defensive in nature.

5. An advantage of the discount rate is that the Fed has the initiative.

6. An advantage of open-market operations is that they are easily reversed.

7. Borrowing from the discount window increases when the discount rate is low relative to the federal-funds rate.

-162-

8. The Fed changes the discount rate frequently, say, once a month.

9. Lowering the discount rate is always a sign of expansionary policy on the part of the Fed.

10. Increases in the discount rate have less political fallout than decreases.

Self-Test: Multiple Choice

1. The Fed's most important and frequently used tool is
   a. moral suasion.
   b. open-market operations.
   c. the discount rate.
   d. the reserve-requirement ratio.
   e. changing the margin requirement.

2. All of the following are selective tools of the Fed *except*
   a. moral suasion.
   b. Regulation Q.
   c. the discount rate.
   d. the margin requirement.
   e. control over consumer credit during World War II.

3. For its open-market operations the Fed is permitted to buy and sell
   a. banker's acceptances.
   b. state and local government securities.
   c. securities of U.S. government agencies.
   d. Ginnie Mae bonds.
   e. All of the above.

4. If the Fed wishes to pursue an anti-inflationary policy, it will probably
   a. sell securities.
   b. buy securities.
   c. lower the discount rate.
   d. lower the reserve-requirement ratio.
   e. decrease the margin requirement.

5. If the Fed buys securities in the open market,
   a. the money supply will increase.
   b. the money supply will decrease.
   c. aggregate demand will increase.
   d. aggregate demand will decrease.
   e. *a* and *c*.
   f. *c* and *d*.

6. If the Fed wishes to decrease the overall level of reserves it will
   a. buy securities.
   b. use one of its selective controls.
   c. use one of its general controls.
   d. sell securities.
   e. c and d.

7. The August 29, 1983, edition of the *Wall Street Journal* reported that the Fed would maintain its moderately restrictive policy for at least several more weeks. The Fed probably (bought/sold) securities, which (quickened/slowed) the growth of the money supply and pushed interest rates (up/down) in the short run.
   a. bought; slowed; up
   b. sold; quickened; up
   c. sold; slowed; up
   d. sold; quickened; down
   e. bought; slowed; down

8. If the Fed wishes to increase the money supply it would (buy/sell) securities, which would (raise/lower) bond prices.
   a. buy; raise
   b. buy; lower
   c. sell; raise
   d. sell; lower

9. The reserve-requirement ratio
   a. is the same for all banks.
   b. works by affecting the money multiplier.
   c. is changed frequently.
   d. is a flexible tool.
   e. serves to protect depositors.

10. Which of the following tools has no announcement effect?
   a. discount rate
   b. margin requirement
   c. moral suasion
   d. open-market operations
   e. All of these tools have announcement effects.

Topics for Discussion

1. What is the difference between defensive and dynamic operations? Which is more visible to the public?

2. What are repos and when are they likely to be used? Give specific examples.

3. Why are changes in the reserve-requirement ratio so seldom used?

4. Why does the Fed deal mainly in Treasury bills as opposed to other securities?

5. Explain why the announcement effect of changes in the discount rate can be ambiguous.

6. What is the difference between general and selective tools? Do general tools have an equal impact on all sectors of the economy?

Exercise Questions

1. The August 4, 1983, edition of the *Wall Street Journal* reported that "The Federal Reserve, seeking to offset the expansionary effect of U.S. intervention in foreign-exchange markets, is using its domestic operations to maintain the monetary restraint it began last May," according to Fed chairman Paul Volcker.

   a. Mr. Volcker is describing (dynamic/defensive) operations.

   b. The Fed probably used (repos/matched sale purchases) to offset its foreign currency intervention.

   c. The federal-funds rate probably (rose/fell) in response to the Fed's domestic market operations.

   d. In response to the Fed's domestic market operations, bond prices probably (rose/fell).

2. Label each of the following actions as generally contractionary or generally expansionary on the part of the Fed.

   a. A rise in the discount rate.

   b. The Fed executes a matched sale purchase.

   c. The Fed extends reserve requirements to cover institutions not currently subject to reserve requirements.

   d. A decrease in the margin requirement.

   e. The Fed increases the maximum maturity of loans for consumer durables.

3. The T account in Table 20.1 represents the balance sheet of the Rat's Haven National Bank. Suppose the Fed buys $1,000 of securities from Rat's Haven. Show how this purchase (increases/decreases) reserves.

Table 20.1 T Account for Rat's Haven National Bank before Fed Purchase

Assets		Liabilities and Net Worth	
Cash	$1,000	Demand deposits	$5,000
Reserves at the Fed	$2,000	Time deposits	$1,200
Securities	$1,000		
Other gunk	. . . . . .	Other gunk	. . . . . .

In Table 20.2, fill in the T account after the Fed buys securities.

Table 20.2 T Account for Rat's Haven National Bank after Fed Purchase

Assets		Liabilities and Net Worth	
Cash	$____	Demand deposits	$____
Reserves at the Fed	$____	Time deposits	$____
Securities	$____		
Other gunk	. . . . . .	Other gunk	. . . . . .

Answers to Self-Tests

Completion

1. reverse repos or matched sale purchases
2. "make a market"
3. defensive
4. adjustment
5. general; selective
6. extended
7. discounting
8. margin
9. moral suasion
10. decreases

True–False

1. False		6. True
2. False		7. True
3. True		8. False
4. True		9. False
5. False		10. False

Multiple Choice

1. *b*	6. *e*
2. *c*	7. *c*
3. *e*	8. *a*
4. *a*	9. *b*
5. *e*	10. *e*

Answers to Exercise Questions

1*a.* defensive
 b. matched sale purchases
 c. rose
 d. fell

2*a.* generally contractionary
 b. generally contractionary
 c. generally contractionary
 d. generally expansionary
 e. generally expansionary

3. increases
  The Fed pays for the securities by increasing Rat's Haven's reserves at the Fed.

Answer to Table 20.2   T Account for Rat's Haven National Bank after Fed Purchase

Assets		Liabilities and Net Worth	
Cash	$1,000	Demand deposits	$5,000
Reserves at the Fed	$3,000	Time deposits	$1,200
Securities	$ 0		
Other gunk	. . . . . .	Other gunk	. . . . . .

CHAPTER 21   The Fed's Targets and Instruments

Learning Objectives

After studying this chapter, you should be able to

1. understand the relationships between tools, instruments, targets, and goals.

2. use the Cambridge equation to explain when the Fed should focus on the money supply and when it should focus on interest rates.

3. use the IS-LM model to explain when the Fed should focus on the money supply and when it should focus on the interest rate.

4. explain why many economists prefer a nonaccommodating policy and why the Fed has become increasingly accommodative.

5. explain why the Fed's deemphasis of money targets, the switch to borrowed reserve and federal-funds instruments, and the apparent use of a real GNP target are all consistent.

Key Terms, Concepts, and Institutions

You should be able to define or explain

targets	lags in monetary control
instruments	interest-rate target
unborrowed reserves	money-stock target
measurability	outstanding credit
controllability	aggregates
relatedness	control theory
target consistency	nominal income target
straddle	real income target
credit rationing	accommodating policy
expected real interest rate	borrowed reserves

Self-Test: Completion

1. The set of variables closely related to the Fed's goals are called

    _____ .

2. Monetarists prefer the _____ as a target since they believe

    _____ is a stable function of known variables.

3. Perhaps the most serious problem in measuring the interest rate is
   that we are not interested in the nominal interest rate but the

    _____ rate of interest.

4. The shift in emphasis from nominal income to real income may
   help explain the continued deemphasis of money as a target

    because money is more closely related to _____ income.

5. The fact that *M-1* tends to grow more rapidly in _____ suggests the Fed is following an accommodative policy.

6. The text speculates that the Fed has been accommodative in an

    attempt to avoid fluctuations in _____ .

7. The Fed usually does not know the money demand function
   exactly so it is difficult to select two consistent money-stock
   and interest-rate targets. They therefore pick ranges for each

    target hoping to _____ a consistent point.

8. It has been argued that choosing any one target is a mistake since
   the behavior of several economic variables gives us information
   about the economy. The theory that tries to predict how each

    variable should be responded to is called _____ theory.

9. If the IS curve shifts out unexpectedly then a(n) _____
   target is appropriate.

10. Given a change in the Cambridge *k* a(n) _____ target is
    appropriate.

11. Different reserve and base concepts are referred to collectively as

     the _____ .

12. The wide range of money definitions means that money does not

     fulfill the _____ criteria for a good target particularly well.

13. If the Cambridge *k* is stable, or a stable function of known vari-

     ables, then money does fulfill the _____ criteria for a good
     target.

-169-

14. If the Phillips curve is vertical, then the interest rate does not fulfill the _____ criteria for a good target.

15. Ben Friedman has argued that the Fed should include outstanding _____ as one of the variables they watch while deciding on monetary policy.

16. In periods of tight money, rather than fully raise interest rates, banks will sometimes meet the credit needs of their preferred long-term customers by cutting off others. This is called

    _____ .

Self-Test: True–False

1. Instruments are more closely related to goals than tools.

2. The use of unattainable targets provides a bureaucracy with an excuse for failure.

3. The Fed can achieve any combination of interest rates and money growth it desires.

4. It is easy to determine the applicable tax rate for the marginal borrower.

5. If the price level is stable, the distinction between the nominal and expected real rate of interest is not a significant problem.

6. Most economists think the short-term interest rate has more effect on investment than the long-term interest rate.

7. We can illustrate the effect of an interest-rate target by drawing a horizontal LM curve.

8. Using a money-stock target allows the crowding-out effect to act as an automatic stabilizer given a shift in the IS curve.

9. If unexpected shifts in the IS and LM curves are equally likely then the interest rate is a better target than the money stock.

10. Total reserves and unborrowed reserves are accurately measurable.

11. According to control theory, we ought to respond to unexpected shifts in the money stock or interest rates by attempting to find out what caused the shifts and then design a control strategy based on that information.

12. If the Fed used a nominal income target, there would be no need for a money-stock or interest-rate target.

13. If nominal income is kept constant and wage demands lead to higher prices then output and employment increase.

14. It may be politically easier to announce a money-stock target than an income target if the Fed's income target is considered too low by the public.

15. If the Fed were to hook the discount rate to the federal-funds rate, policy would be less accommodative.

Self-Test: Multiple Choice

1. The Fed's use of borrowed reserves as an instrument
   a. increases the Fed's control over money.
   b. allows an increase in money demand to increase money supply.
   c. is universally applauded by economists.
   d. fights inflation because an increase in prices will force up money demand and interest rates.
   e. allows variations in money demand to affect interest rates and income.

2. The Fed should use an interest-rate target when
   a. prices are rising rapidly.
   b. government expenditure is rising rapidly.
   c. investment falls as businessmen lose confidence.
   d. k changes.
   e. a, b, and c.

3. Under an interest-rate target, an increase in government spending
   a. still crowds out private investment in the short run.
   b. results in a smaller change in nominal income than under a money-stock target.
   c. results in a larger change in nominal income than under a money-stock target.
   d. leaves nominal income unchanged.
   e. forces the Fed to sell government bonds.

4. Under a money-stock target, an increase in government spending
   a. forces the Fed to buy government bonds.
   b. crowds out private investment in the short run.
   c. leaves nominal income unchanged.
   d. causes nominal income to rise but by less than that under an interest-rate target.
   e. Both b and d.

5. An increase in the Cambridge k
   a. under a money-stock target leads to lower interest rates and a lower nominal income.
   b. leaves income and interest rates unchanged under an interest-rate target.
   c. under a money-stock target leads to higher interest rates and a higher nominal income.
   d. still reduces income under an interest-rate target but not by as much as under a money-stock target.
   e. could be due to a higher price level.

6. All of the following are problems with the measurement of interest rates *except*
   a. credit rationing.
   b. measuring the expected rate of inflation.
   c. constructing an appropriate average.
   d. estimating the impact of taxes.
   e. the vertical Phillips curve.

7. If the long-run Phillips curve is vertical, then any attempt by the Fed to raise output above the natural rate by lowering interest rates will
   a. result in only a temporary reduction in interest rates. The long-run effect will be an increase in the price level.
   b. create a recession.
   c. permanently increase investment, growth, and income.
   d. increase prices in the short run but not the long run.
   e. reduce prices and increase income.

8. One of the major criticisms of the Fed over the last few decades is that
   a. money growth has been procyclical.
   b. the Fed has given excessive attention to the aggregates.
   c. it has been unwilling to exercise independent judgment.
   d. it has refused to help the Treasury finance deficits by buying Treasury bills.
   e. by openly discussing the reasons for their decisions it has politicized monetary policy.

9. From a political point of view it might be better to target
   a. money than interest rates because it may be easier to "sell" a necessary restrictive policy by emphasizing the slow money growth than by pointing to the higher interest rates.
   b. money than interest rates because focusing on money emphasizes short-term goals.
   c. interest rates than money because interest rates measure the value of money and the Fed's primary mission is to stabilize money's value.

d. real income than nominal income because it is usually more popular to accommodate price increases than fight them.

e. Both *a* and *d.*

10. Measurement problems include
    a. the difference between real and nominal interest rates.
    b. seasonal corrections of the money supply data.
    c. whether *M-1, M-2,* or some weighted aggregate is the appropriate target.
    d. pre-tax versus after-tax interest rates.
    e. All of the above.

Topics for Discussion

The September 15, 1986, *Wall Street Journal* ran an article on page one titled "The Fed Can't Avoid Erring Toward Ease." Use what you have learned in this chapter to discuss the following paraphrased excerpts.

1. While the public stoically accepted the high interest rates needed to fight inflation in 1981–82, they, and their elected representatives, would oppose a recession now.

2. According to Charles Partee, a former Board member, the Fed will not allow a recession unless they have a good excuse.

3. The recent stock market plunge was linked to fears that inflation might revive.

4. Fed policymakers don't think they are risking renewed inflation. Wage gains are the weakest in decades and the economy is growing slowly.

5. Stephen Axilrod, a former top staffer, frets that the decline in the dollar's value will eventually boost demand for exports and increase the price of imports, rekindling inflation.

6. *M-1* growth over the last 6 months has been 17.9 percent.

7. Long-term interest rates have been edging upward while the Fed has cut the discount rate three times.

8. You have the advantage that much time has passed since this was written. Who was right, the Fed or its critics?

Exercise Questions

Interest-Rate and Money-Stock Targets Compared. For Exercises 1–3 we have the usual IS-LM curves. The curves intersect at the desired level of output. There is also an LM* curve that represents equilibrium in the money market under an interest-rate target. Such a curve assumes the Fed expands or contracts the money supply to keep the interest rate constant. While the LM* is technically not an LM curve, since such a curve assumes a constant money stock, it is a useful device.

1. Assume investors lose confidence and invest less.

   a. Shift the appropriate curve in Figure 21.1 in the correct direction. Compare the new point of intersection of IS and LM, which would be the equilibrium given a money-stock target, with the point on LM*, which would be the new equilibrium given an interest-rate target.

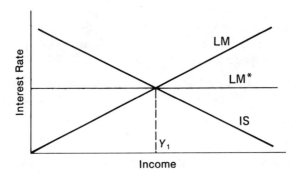

Figure 21.1 IS-LM Curves

Under the interest-rate target, the change in income is (*b.* larger/ smaller) than under a money-stock target. So (*c.* an interest-rate/ a money-stock) target is better.

2. Assume new types of accounts increase money demand.

   a. Shift the appropriate curve in Figure 21.2 in the correct direction. Compare the new point of intersection of IS on LM, which would be the equilibrium given a money-stock target, with the point on LM*, the new equilibrium given an interest-rate target.

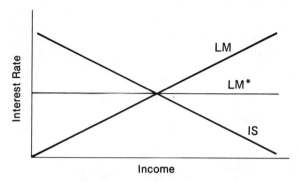

Figure 21.2 IS-LM Curves

Under the interest-rate target, the change in income is (*b:* larger/ smaller) than under a money-stock target. So (*c:* an interest-rate/ a money-stock) target is better.

3. Assume government spending increases.

a. Shift the appropriate curve in Figure 21.3 in the correct direc- tion. Compare the new point of intersection of IS on LM, which would be the equilibrium given a money-stock target, with the point on LM*, the new equilibrium given an interest- rate target.

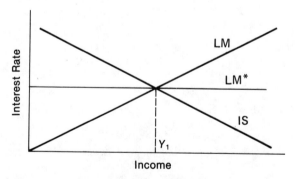

Figure 21.3 IS-LM Curves

Under the interest-rate target the change in income is (*b:* larger/ smaller) than under a money-stock target. So (*c:* an interest-rate/ a money-stock) target is better.

Answers to Self-Tests

Completion

1. targets
2. money stock, k
3. expected real
4. nominal
5. expansions
6. interest rates
7. straddle
8. control
9. money stock
10. interest rate
11. aggregates
12. measurability
13. relatedness
14. controllability
15. credit (or debt)
16. credit rationing

True–False

1. False
2. True
3. False
4. False
5. True
6. False
7. True
8. True
9. False
10. True
11. True
12. False
13. False
14. True
15. True

Multiple Choice

1. *b*
2. *d*
3. *c*
4. *e*
5. *b*
6. *e*
7. *a*
8. *a*
9. *e*
10. *e*

Answers to Exercise Questions

1a.

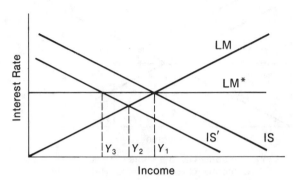

Y₂ = Income Given a Money Stock
Y₃ = Income Given an Interest Rate Target

Answer to Figure 21.1 IS-LM Curves

b. larger
c. money stock

2a.

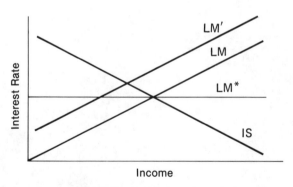

Answer to Figure 21.2 IS-LM Curves

b. smaller
c. interest rate

3a.

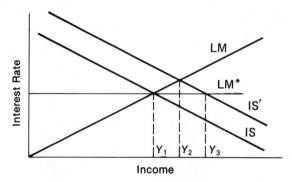

Income

Y_2 = Income Given a Money Stock
Y_3 = Income Given an Interest Rate Target

Answer to Figure 21.3   IS-LM Curves

b. larger
c. money stock

CHAPTER 22　The Impact of Monetary Policy

Learning Objectives

After studying this chapter, you should be able to

1. describe the monetarist transmission mechanism and how it differs from the Keynesian mechanism.

2. discuss the impact of money-market imperfections on the strength of monetary policy.

3. describe the process by which monetary policy affects consumption and stock prices.

4. describe how the MPS model works through its three channels.

5. explain how monetary policy affects income through its effects on international trade.

6. use the monetarist balance-of-payments theory to explain how a restrictive monetary policy can curb inflation.

7. explain the implications of rational expectations theory for monetary policy.

8. explain the potential impact that a flexible interest rate on transactions accounts may have on monetary and fiscal policy.

9. list which sectors of the economy are hardest hit by restrictive monetary policy and why.

Key Terms, Concepts, and Institutions

You should be able to define or explain

portfolio equilibrium
monetarist transmission process
trade credit
MPS model
wealth effect
cost of capital channel

credit availability channel
equilibrium quasi-rent
monetarist balance-of-payments
    theory
rational expectations
credit allocation

Self-Test: Completion

1. When the quantity of money increases, the yield on money (increases/decreases).

2. The payment of a flexible interest rate on money makes income _____ stable with respect to a shift in the IS curve.

3. If the Fed pursues a noninflationary expansionary monetary policy, stock prices will (rise/fall).

4. According to the monetarist transmission mechanism, a fall in the money stock will (raise/lower) the prices of all assets in the economy.

5. _____ theorists believe that an increase in the rate of growth of the monetary base could lead to an immediate increase in prices if people expect it to and react accordingly.

6. The slope of the _____ curve determines how responsive interest rates are to changes in the money stock.

7. Residential construction is hurt severely by restrictive monetary policy because it is a _____ investment.

8. The credit a firm extends by shipping goods to another firm with payment to be made in the future is called _____.

9. As interest rates rise in the United States, the increased purchases of U.S. securities by foreigners work to moderate the rise in the interest rate, which (enhances/reduces) the impact of the Fed's (expansionary/restrictive) policy.

10. The yield firms must expect to obtain on investment in industrial plants to make them willing to undertake such investments is called the _____.

Self-Test: True–False

1. The MPS model is essentially a Keynesian model.

2. According to the monetarists, an increase in the money supply spurs investment because the value of existing corporations exceeds the cost of creating new ones.

3. The empirical evidence suggests that the existence of trade credit weakens the impact of restrictive monetary policy.

4. In the long run, a system of credit allocation is ineffective.

5. When U.S. interest rates rise, the prices of imported goods also rise.

6. The payment of a flexible interest rate on money makes income more stable with respect to changes in the LM curve.

7. Most Keynesians believe that monetary policy would have no impact during a severe recession.

8. An increase in interest rates is likely to depress stock prices.

9. A rise in the corporate-bond rate increases the flow of deposits to thrift institutions.

10. A rise in the Aaa-bond rate raises mortgage rates because bonds and mortgages are complements.

Self-Test: Multiple Choice

1. A restrictive monetary policy hits the residential construction industry so hard because
   a. the value of houses declines.
   b. interest costs on long-term investments are a large part of total costs.
   c. the value of the dollar rises when interest rates are high.
   d. the Fed uses its selective tools to restrict credit to the housing industry.
   e. usury laws push interest rates up too high.

2. Select the correct statement regarding the strength of monetary policy.
   a. Most economists believe that changes in the money stock have very little effect on GNP.
   b. The predominant view is that monetary policy cannot terminate a really severe recession.
   c. Restrictive monetary policy can bring about a recession.

-181-

    d. Expansionary monetary policy can bring about a recovery.

    e. Changes in the money stock are mostly offset by changes in the velocity of money.

3. According to the monetarists, decreases in the money stock

    a. decrease investment by increasing interest rates.

    b. decrease the yield on money.

    c. decrease investment because the value of existing corporations exceeds the cost of creating new ones.

    d. lower the prices of all assets in the economy.

    e. increase the imputed yield on consumer durables.

4. According to the monetarist balance-of-payments theory, if the Fed adopts an expansionary monetary policy

    a. prices in the United States will be reduced directly and indirectly, as those producers who compete against imported goods have to reduce their prices.

    b. the price of foreign currency in terms of dollars rises.

    c. the price of internationally traded goods in terms of dollars rises.

    d. the dollar falls.

    e. All of the above.

5. A fall in interest rates

    a. gives households an incentive to hold more consumer durables.

    b. encourages households to buy more securities since their prices will rise in the future.

    c. decreases household liquidity.

    d. encourages households to purchase imported goods.

    e. *a* and *d.*

6. Suppose you have inside information that the Fed intends to pursue a restrictive monetary policy in the next few months. You should

    a. buy stocks.

    b. sell stocks.

    c. buy foreign currency.

    d. sell dollars.

    e. *b* and *c.*

7. In the Fed's MPS model, the quantity of money affects income through

    a. wealth effects.

    b. credit availability effects.

    c. changes in the yield available on money.

    d. changes in the prices of other assets.

    e. *a* and *b.*

8. A rise in the yield on Treasury securities
   a. increases the Aaa-bond yield.
   b. increases mortgage yields.
   c. decreases housing starts.
   d. decreases investment in industrial plants.
   e. All of the above.

9. If U.S. interest rates fall
   a. the value of the dollar in terms of foreign currencies rises.
   b. the value of the dollar in terms of foreign currencies falls.
   c. U.S. goods cost more in terms of foreign currencies.
   d. imports rise.
   e. a, c, and d.

10. The payment of an explicit rate of interest on money that varies
    with market rates of interest
    a. causes the liquidity preference curve to become flatter.
    b. causes the LM curve to be flatter.
    c. makes income more stable with respect to a shift in the IS
       curve.
    d. gives households an incentive to reduce their holdings of
       securities when interest rates fall.
    e. None of the above.

Topics for Discussion

1. Describe the effects of a restrictive monetary policy according to
   the monetarist scenario.

2. Why are market imperfections less likely to impact on monetary
   policy in the future?

3. How could an increase in the money supply decrease stock
   prices?

4. Describe how the effect of monetary policy on international
   trade reinforces domestic effects.

5. Consider the direction of impact of the second-round effects in
   the MPS model. Is the direction the same for first- and second-
   round effects?

6. What sectors of the economy (besides residential construction
   and small businesses) are hurt by restrictive monetary policy?

Exercise Questions

Although somebody spilled coffee on these clippings from the Wall Street Journal, *you should be able to decipher them with the hints provided.*

1. "The dollar rose in Europe yesterday on expectations that short-term U.S. interest rates would stay at current levels or move (higher/lower). But the U.S. Federal Reserve later 'surprised the market' by injecting reserves into the banking network, (raising/lowering) the dollar in New York, said Frank Pasateri, an assistant vice-president of Bank America International." (*Wall Street Journal*, September 1, 1983)

2. "New home sales declined 6.5 percent in July as this summer's steep (rise/decline) in mortgage interest rates took its toll." (*Wall Street Journal*, August 30, 1983)

3. "The nation's merchandise trade deficit widened sharply in July to $6.36 billion, reflecting the vigorous U.S. recovery and the (strength/weakness) of the dollar, the Commerce Department said. . . . The dollar's (strength/weakness) has (enhanced/reduced) the competitiveness of U.S. exports on world markets by making American goods (cheaper/more expensive) for foreign currency holders." (*Wall Street Journal*, August 30, 1983)

4. "Fear of higher interest rates pushed (up/down) bonds and stocks. . . . The dollar (rebounded/declined)." (*Wall Street Journal*, August 19, 1983)

Answers to Self-Tests

Completion

1. decreases
2. more
3. rise
4. lower
5. rational expectations
6. liquidity preference
7. long-term
8. trade credit
9. reduces; restrictive
10. equilibrium quasi-rent

True–False

1. True	6. False
2. True	7. False
3. False	8. True
4. True	9. False
5. False	10. False

Multiple Choice

1. *b*	6. *b*
2. *b*	7. *e*
3. *d*	8. *e*
4. *b*	9. *b*
5. *a*	10. *c*

Answers to Exercise Questions

1. higher; lowering
2. rise
3. strength; strength; reduced; more expensive
4. down; rebounded

CHAPTER 23   Can Countercyclical Monetary Policy Succeed?

Learning Objectives

After studying this chapter, you should be able to

1. explain why policy increases the variance of the income path even if the effects of policy on income and the naturally occurring deviations in income are not correlated.

2. recognize the difficulties that lags in the effect of policy produce.

3. recognize that the economy moves through time and that our static models seriously understate the difficulties involved in returning an economy to the equilibrium level of employment.

4. explain and evaluate the rational expectations hypothesis.

5. explore some of the political and administrative problems that inhibit stabilization policy.

Key Terms, Concepts, and Institutions

You should be able to define or explain

countercyclical policy
variance
correlation
distributed lag
inside lag

outside lag
implicit contract
rational expectations
expected money growth
Fed as a whipping boy

Self-Test: Completion

1. The square of the standard deviation of a variable about its trend is known as the _____.

· 2. The impact of monetary policy on nominal income is felt gradually over time. This is called the _____ of policy.

3. While estimates of the impact of monetary policy vary considerably, most agree it takes at least _____ quarters for policy to achieve half of its ultimate effect.

4. The time between recognition of the need for corrective action and the Fed's corrective action is called the _____ lag.

5. The time between taking the corrective action and its impact is called the _____ lag.

6. Instead of looking at the policy tool's strength, one should use that tool with the most _____ impact.

7. The Fed may find it useful to avoid clearly stating _____ so that the Fed can convince various interest groups that their interests are given sufficient importance.

8. One of the Keynesian justifications for countercyclical policy is that wages are _____.

9. The rational expectations approach blames unemployment on _____.

10. If workers and employers informally agree not to take advantage of every variation in the marketplace and wait to renegotiate contracts based on more fundamental changes, then the _____ theory is correct.

11. Some rational expectations theorists have argued that only a(n) _____ increase in money growth will increase nominal income even temporarily.

Self-Test: True–False

1. If the correlation coefficient between stabilization policy and income is between 0 and –1, then the policy should be strong

enough that the variance of policy's effects equals the variance of the natural income path.

2. If policy is equally likely to add or subtract 1 percent to nominal income at a cyclical peak, then the variance of nominal income is unaffected by policy.

3. The inside lag can be negative.

4. Since the effects of policy occur over time, if the Fed wants to rapidly achieve any particular goal it will find itself taking measures to counteract its past policy once the goal is reached.

5. There is some limited evidence that suggests the outside lag of monetary policy is highly variable.

6. Stronger tools, even if their impact is somewhat less predictable, are better tools.

7. According to the rational expectations theory, new policies based on an examination of past behavior have a weak foundation given that people may change their behavior in response to the new policy.

8. If people come to expect tax reductions in recessions and tax increases in inflations, then the change in consumption due to the tax changes will be larger.

9. One possible explanation of the fact that prices are now rising in recessions is that people expect countercyclical policy during a recession.

10. The rational expectations theory explains periods of unemployment by saying it takes time for employers and workers to recognize that the demand shifts they see in their own industries are both long lasting and the result of an aggregate-demand shift and not just a change in relative demand.

11. According to rational expectations theory, people will react no differently to announced changes in aggregate demand than to unannounced changes.

12. Since rational expectations theory implies policy can have no systematic effect, stabilization policy leaves the variance of nominal income no larger and no smaller than it would be in the absence of stabilization policy.

13. It is costly for individuals to learn what sort of monetary policy helps them most. Since their chance of successfully influencing policy is small they may rationally choose to remain ignorant.

14. One way to explain the rational expectations hypothesis is to notice that people are not rocks. While you may be able to repeatedly hit a rock with a hammer, the only way you will be able to pound a person is if it is unexpected.

15. A car with a distributed lag steering mechanism would be easy to control.

Self-Test: Multiple Choice

1. Assume it takes the Fed about one quarter of recessionary experience to initiate countercyclical policy. Given the average postwar recession of _____ months and the fact it takes at least _____ quarters for half of the impact of policy to be felt, we can say most of the impact of policy will be felt _____ the recession.
   a. 20; 8; after
   b. 30; 4; during
   c. 10; 2; after
   d. 5; 1; during
   e. 45; 20; after

2. Stabilization policy is likely to be more successful if
   a. monetary policy has a strong effect on income.
   b. the outside lag is long.
   c. expectations are rational.
   d. we can predict nominal income accurately.
   e. the Fed delays action until a strong consensus forms.

3. The inside lag would be shorter if
   a. the Fed began to take action to offset predicted deviations in income.
   b. investment responded more quickly to changes in the rate of interest.
   c. long-term interest rates responded more quickly to changes in the short-term rate of interest.
   d. prices were more flexible.
   e. All of the above.

4. Which of the following potential political or administrative problems is discussed in the text?
   a. Special-interest groups may dominate decision-making.
   b. The Fed may pursue its own bureaucratic interests.

c. The electorate may be uninformed.
d. The Fed may concentrate on the short-term problems.
e. All of the above.

5. According to the rational expectations argument, unemployment is caused by
   a. the difference between planned and actual investment.
   b. the low level of planned investment.
   c. inflexible prices.
   d. the fact that different inputs become fully employed at different levels of income.
   e. the fact that it takes time for unemployment and a general lack of demand to be considered persistent.

6. According to the rational expectations argument, an announced increase in the supply of money
   a. will have no effect on real income.
   b. is equally likely to increase as reduce real income since people are as likely to overcorrect for the stimulus as undercorrect.
   c. will always increase real income because of implicit contracts.
   d. will have a bigger impact on real income than an unannounced increase in the supply of money.
   e. will reduce real income.

7. The implicit contract theory refers to
   a. the drug trade.
   b. mutual loyalty arrangements between workers and employers.
   c. cost-of-living escalators in union contracts.
   d. agreements among workers not to break an informally arranged pace of work.
   e. agreements among workers not to cross each other's picket lines.

8. Not all the implications of rational expectations are negative. Announcement effects could help
   a. by increasing the impact of a tax cut that is described as temporary.
   b. because an expected increase in the money supply has a more predictable effect than an unexpected increase.
   c. because an announced anti-inflation policy may need less unemployment to reduce inflation.
   d. because an announced increase in government spending is more likely to raise real income than prices.
   e. because if everyone knows the money stock will be increased in a recession, recessions will not occur.

9. Robert Hetzel argues that Congress could reduce the Fed's independence if the Fed pursued distasteful policies. To avoid this the Fed
   a. demands that the Congress state explicit goals for the Fed to follow.
   b. clearly states its goals to avoid confusion.
   c. avoids clearly stated policies, goals, or methods of analysis in order to avoid conflict.
   d. emphasizes future GNP over current GNP.
   e. moves quickly and decisively on the basis of preliminary data.

10. If the distributed lag of the effect of monetary policy is long and variable, then
    a. the correlation coefficient between policy and the natural income path cannot be negative.
    b. expectations are not rational.
    c. policy taken to end a bust could end up accentuating a boom.
    d. countercyclical policy is always harmful.
    e. countercyclical policy is always beneficial.

Topics for Discussion

While Chapter 23 argues that Keynes's ambition to use monetary policy to stabilize the economy on a continuous basis was a vain hope, there is more to his writing. In this regard, the following quotes from The Collected Writings of John Maynard Keynes *are worth considering.*

1. "Many of the greatest economic evils of our time are the fruits of risk, uncertainty, and ignorance. It is because particular individuals, fortunate in situation or in abilities, are able to take advantage of uncertainty and ignorance, and also because for the same reason big business is often a lottery, that great inequalities of wealth come about; and these same factors are also the cause of the unemployment of labour, or the disappointment of reasonable business expectations, and of the impairment of efficiency and production. Yet the cure lies outside the operations of individuals; it may even be to the interest of individuals to aggravate the disease. I believe that the cure for these things is partly to be sought in the deliberate control of the currency and of credit by a central institution, and partly in the collection and dissemination on a great scale of data relating to the business situation, includ-

ing the full publicity, by law if necessary, of all business facts which it is useful to know."[1]

2. "Furthermore, it seems unlikely that the influence of banking policy on the rate of interest will be sufficient by itself to determine an optimum rate of investment. I conceive, therefore, that a somewhat comprehensive socialization of investment will prove the only means of securing an approximation to full employment; though this need not exclude all manner of compromises and of devices by which public authority will cooperate with private initiative. But beyond this no obvious case is made out for a system of State Socialism which would embrace most of the economic life of the community. It is not the ownership of the instruments of production which it is important for the State to assume. If the State is able to determine the aggregate amount of resources devoted to augmenting the instruments and the basic rate of reward to those who own them, it will have accomplished all that is necessary."[2]

3. "The full employment policy by means of investment is only one particular application of an intellectual theorem. You can produce the result just as well by consuming more or working less. Personally I regard the investment policy as first aid. In U.S. it almost certainly will not do the trick. Less work is the ultimate solution (a 35-hour week would do the trick now)."[3]

4. "Moderate planning will be safe if those carrying it out are rightly oriented in their own minds and hearts to the moral issue. . . . But the curse is that there is also an important section who could almost be said to want planning not in order to enjoy its fruits but because morally they hold ideas exactly the opposite of yours, and wish to serve not God but the devil."[4]

[1] Keynes, John Maynard. *The Collected Writings of John Maynard Keynes.* Volume 9: *Essays in Persuasion.* London: Macmillan; NY: St. Martins Press for the Royal Economic Society, 1972, p. 292.

[2] Keynes, John Maynard. *The Collected Writings of John Maynard Keynes.* Volume 7: *The General Theory of Employment Interest and Money.* London: Macmillan; NY: St. Martins Press for the Royal Economic Society, 1973, p. 378.

[3] Keynes, John Maynard. *The Collected Writings of John Maynard Keynes.* Volume 27: *Activities 1940-1946 Shaping the Post War World: Employment and Commodities.* Ed.: Donald Moggridge. London: Macmillan; NY: Cambridge University Press for the Royal Economic Society, 1980, p. 384.

[4] Keynes, John Maynard. *The Collected Writings of John Maynard Keynes.* Volume 27: *Activities 1940-1946 Shaping the Post War World: Employment and Commodities.* Ed.: Donald Moggridge. London: Macmillan; NY: Cambridge University Press for the Royal Economic Society, 1980, p. 387.

5. "The time may arrive a little later when the community as a whole must pay attention to the innate quality as well as to the mere numbers of its future members."[5]

Exercise Questions

1. The error-learning model used to be a popular way of describing expectations formation until the rational expectations theorists showed that it led to systematic errors. As you work through this exercise you'll see why.

   Assume some variable has been rising at a 5 percent rate for the last few months and slows to 4 percent. The error-learning model will project next month's growth rate to be (*a:* greater than/less than/equal to) 4 percent. The growth rates for the following months turn out to be 2 percent, then 1 percent, then −1 percent. Someone using an error-learning model will consistently predict growth rates that are (*b:* higher than/lower than/equal to) the actual rate. Someone with rational expectations (*c:* will/ will not) guess at the turning points between growth and decline and (*d:* will/will not) use the experience of past cycles to make guesses that (*e:* are more precise/while they may be just as imprecise avoid systematic error).

2. In order to illustrate the variance formula let income be $4 billion above the desired trend one year, $4 billion below trend the next year, $4 billion above trend the third year, and, finally, $4 billion below trend the fourth year. Policy adds $1 billion to income the first two years and subtracts $1 billion from income the final two years. If we let x represent the deviations from trend of the natural income path, y represent the impact of policy on the deviations of income, and z represent their sum, we have

$$x = +4 -4 +4 -4$$
$$y = +1 +1 -1 -1$$
$$z = +5 -3 +3 -5.$$

   a. Add up the absolute value of all the numbers in the series x and divide by 4. This is the average absolute deviation.

   b. Using the same technique, find the average absolute deviation of z.

[5] Keynes, John Maynard. *The Collected Writings of John Maynard Keynes.* Volume 9: *Essays in Persuasion.* London: Macmillan; NY: St. Martins Press for the Royal Economic Society, 1972, p. 292.

c. If the goal of policy is to minimize the average absolute deviation of income, has policy been harmful?

d. Calculate the variances of the series x, y, and z. This can be done by summing the squares of the entries in each series and dividing the total by 4.

e. If the goal of policy is to minimize the variance of income, has policy been harmful?

f. Notice that the variance of z equals the sum of the variances of x and y. What does this imply about the correlation of x and y? (Hint: Use the formula presented on page 363 of the text.)

g. Explain why your answer in *f* makes sense.

Answers to Self-Tests

Completion

1. variance
2. distributed lag
3. two
4. inside
5. outside
6. predictable
7. goals
8. sticky
9. forecast errors
10. implicit contract
11. unexpected

True–False

1. False
2. False
3. True
4. True
5. True
6. False
7. True
8. False

9. True
10. True
11. False
12. False
13. True
14. True
15. False

Multiple Choice

1. *c*	6. *b*
2. *d*	7. *b*
3. *a*	8. *c*
4. *e*	9. *c*
5. *e*	10. *c*

Answers to Exercise Questions

1*a*. greater than
  b. higher
  c. will
  d. will
  e. while they may be just as imprecise avoid systematic error

2*a*. 4
  b. 4
  c. no
  d. the variance of x is 16
   the variance of y is 1
   the variance of z is 17
  e. yes
  f. The coefficient of correlation between x and y is zero, otherwise the variance of z would not be the simple sum of the variances of x and y.
  g. This makes sense because positive or negative values of x are as likely to be associated with positive values of y as with negative values. Knowing the value of a particular x tells us nothing about the value of the corresponding y.

CHAPTER 24 The Record of Monetary Policy

Learning Objectives

After studying this chapter, you should be able to

1. outline the critical episodes in monetary history since the Fed's inception in 1913.

2. describe how and why the Fed's goals have changed since 1913.

3. evaluate critically the Fed's performance during each of the critical episodes outlined in the text.

Key Terms, Concepts, and Institutions

You should be able to define or explain

real-bills doctrine
eligible paper
pegged interest rates
the Federal Reserve–Treasury
  Accord
rollover

stagflation
base drift
elastic currency
"Saturday night special"
monetarist experiment

Self-Test: Completion

1. According to ⎯⎯⎯⎯⎯, deposit creation cannot be inflationary if deposits are created as a result of short-term self-liquidating loans that finance real activities.

2. ⎯⎯⎯⎯⎯ was the term used for promissory notes banks had discounted for their customers that met the requirements of the real-bills doctrine.

3. According to Milton Friedman and Anna Schwartz, the Fed pursued a _____ policy during the Great Depression.

4. During the Great Depression, the velocity of money _____.

5. According to Peter Temin, the decline in _____ caused the decline in _____.

6. The Fed's policy during World War II was to _____ interest rates.

7. The agreement reached by the Fed and the Treasury in 1951 was called _____.

8. The use of targets such as short-term interest rates and free reserves is procyclical if the _____ curve shifts.

9. From October 6, 1979, till the second half of 1982 Federal Reserve policy was widely interpreted as a _____.

10. The Fed announced its intention to pay more attention to monetary aggregates and less attention to interest rates in _____ (month and year).

Self-Test: True–False

1. The Fed was clearly to blame for the severe recession which began in January of 1920.

2. The Fed first attempted countercyclical monetary policy during the 1920s.

3. The decline in the monetary stock during the Great Depression was due to a decline in the reserve base.

4. For the decade 1929–39, real interest rates exceeded nominal interest rates.

5. Keynesians attribute the decline in the velocity of money which occurred during the Great Depression to low interest rates.

6. Temin argues that the stock of money declined during the Great Depression because income fell and reduced the demand for money.

7. During both world wars the main goal of the Fed was to keep interest rates low to accommodate the Treasury's financing needs.

8. The Fed was in effective control of the money stock during World War II.

9. The rise of the monetarist influence at the Fed traces back to the 1960s.

10. The inflation of the 1960s was primarily due to supply shocks.

Self-Test: Multiple Choice

1. When the Fed was inaugurated in 1913, its *major* goal was
   a. maintenance of the gold standard.
   b. avoiding financial panics.
   c. stabilizing interest rates.
   d. controlling inflation.
   e. All of the above.

2. The decline in the money stock during the Great Depression was due to
   a. a decline in the reserve base.
   b. banks choosing to hold more reserves to deposits.
   c. the public choosing to hold more currency to deposits.
   d. All of the above.
   e. Only *b* and *c*.

3. According to Friedman and Schwartz, the decline in the money stock during the Great Depression was the result of
   a. a shift in the demand for money.
   b. a decrease in income.
   c. an exogenous drop in consumption.
   d. a leftward shift in the supply curve of money.
   e. All of the above except *d*.

4. Temin argues that interest rates were low during the depression because
   a. the demand for liquid securities increased due to the public's unwillingness to hold illiquid assets.
   b. the demand for money decreased.
   c. the money stock increased.
   d. the inflation rate declined.
   e. None of the above.

5. The great debate between the Fed and the Treasury after World War II
   a. resulted in the 1951 agreement known as the Treasury–Federal Reserve Accord.
   b. was over the control of the money stock.

c. pitted the Treasury's desire for low interest rates against the Fed's desire for a tighter policy to combat inflation.

d. resulted in higher short-term interest rates.

e. All of the above.

6. The recovery which started in November of 1982 is unusual because

a. the federal deficit is low.

b. there is a large import deficit.

c. inflation has risen.

d. inflation has not risen.

e. the unemployment rate is extremely low.

7. The Fed's "credit crunch" policy in 1966

a. was blamed for a sharp decrease in residential construction.

b. did not affect the ability of banks and thrifts to buy deposits since Regulation Q ceilings were above market rates of interest.

c. continued through 1971.

d. helped to bring on the 1973–75 recession.

e. All of the above.

8. In the wake of the failure of the Penn Central Transportation Company

a. the Fed imposed wage and price controls.

b. the Fed lowered reserve requirements.

c. the Chrysler Corporation could not roll over its commercial paper.

d. banks were forced to honor phony lines of credit.

e. the Fed raised the Regulation Q ceilings.

9. The bond market collapsed in 1980

a. as a result of the collapse of the mortgage market.

b. because investors feared that interest rates would fall as a result of unprecedented growth in the money stock.

c. because investors feared that inflation, and therefore also interest rates, would skyrocket.

d. because the marginal efficiency of investment shifted inward.

e. due to an unexplained shift in consumption.

10. All of the following were part of President Carter's March 1980 program to break inflationary expectations *except*

a. raising the reserve requirement on certain managed liabilities.

b. imposing a reserve requirement on increase in the assets of money-market funds.

c. imposing a reserve requirement on unsecured consumer loans.

d. instituting mandatory wage and price controls.

e. placing a surcharge on the discount rate paid by large banks which borrowed frequently.

Topics for Discussion

1. Why was it odd for a Democratic president to request that the Fed follow a restrictive monetary policy, as President Carter did in 1978?

2. Discuss in detail how recent financial innovations have clouded the interpretation of *M-1*, and why the Fed has temporarily decided to let *M-1* rise above its target.

3. What is the problem with wage and price controls as an antidote to inflation?

Exercise Questions

1. The *Wall Street Journal* reported on September 13, 1983, another attempt by the Fed to lean against the wind: "Worries about the federal government's huge end-of-the-quarter borrowing operation helped depress bond prices yesterday, erasing some of the large gains registered recently.

   "The bond markets had rallied strongly in the last few weeks because of a sharp slowing in the growth rate of the nation's money supply. With the money measure well within the Federal Reserve System's target range, many analysts contend the central bank may soon be able to ease credit conditions, paving the way for lower interest rates. . . .

   "The Fed began to tighten its credit clamp last May in an effort to keep the economic recovery from becoming overheated. Some analysts say the maneuver worked."

   a. Before the 1951 Federal Reserve–Treasury Accord, what would you have expected the Fed to do in response to the Treasury's borrowing operations?

   b. If the *Journal* had been reporting a similar story before the 1979 monetarist revolution, what measure would the analysts have been watching, as opposed to the money supply?

2. The *Wall Street Journal* reported on October 6, 1986 (p. 1), that "Paul Volcker, who usually speaks last in Federal Reserve policy debates, surprised his colleagues at an important meeting

July 8. The Fed chairman spoke first, and he made it clear that he wanted to lower interest rates.

"Mr. Volcker's comments were particularly striking because just five months earlier, at a February 24 meeting, he had strenuously resisted an interest rate cut. Indeed, he had nearly quit when four Reserve Board members appointed by President Reagan outvoted him, his first such defeat since becoming chairman in 1979."

The article goes on to say that the year 1986 marked a turning point in the Volcker era. Given the Fed's monetary policy since 1979, what is the new emphasis?

Answers to Self-Tests

Completion

1. the real-bills doctrine
2. Eligible paper
3. tight
4. fell
5. income; money stock
6. peg
7. the Accord
8. IS
9. monetarist experiment
10. October 1979

True–False

1. False	6. True
2. True	7. True
3. False	8. False
4. True	9. True
5. True	10. False

Multiple Choice

1. *a*	6. *d*
2. *e*	7. *a*
3. *d*	8. *b*
4. *b*	9. *c*
5. *e*	10. *d*

Answers to Exercise Questions

1*a.* The Fed would have increased the money supply by buying the Treasury's securities at a low rate of interest.

b. Probably the federal-funds rate and other short-term rates.

2. As of this writing (October 1986), Mr. Volcker and other Federal Reserve officials were putting more emphasis on fighting recession and less emphasis on fighting inflation. Prior to this date, Mr. Volcker concentrated primarily on fighting inflation.

CHAPTER 25   Alternative Monetary Standards

Learning Objectives

After studying this chapter, you should be able to

1. argue for a constant money growth-rate rule.

2. argue against a constant money growth-rate rule.

3. explain the interconnections between the money growth-rate rule and the other 11 propositions of monetarism.

4. explain and criticize alternative standards, such as private money, the gold standard, and semi-rules.

Key Terms, Concepts, and Institutions

You should be able to define or explain

second-best policy
political pressure to accommodate stable velocity
evasion
multiple currency standard

political feasibility
semi-rules
gold standard
full-employment approach

Self-Test: Completion

1. Part of the case for the rule is that our imperfect knowledge implies that the correlation coefficient between the initial fluctuation in income and the fluctuation induced by policy may

   be _____ so that policy is _____.

2. The case for a money growth-rate rule was severely undermined in the early 1980s when velocity which had been _____ began to _____.

3. A rule that sets the money growth rate according to an equation containing current and past income growth is known as a

_____.

4. The full-employment approach argues that inflation should be controlled by a(n) _____ policy rather than monetary policy.

5. One of the main arguments against the money growth-rate rule is that prices are _____ and velocity is not _____.

6. As long as the allowable interest rates on deposits are less than the market rate and the Fed does not pay interest on reserves, then if a money growth-rate led to high interest rates there would be an incentive to develop money _____.

7. Some argue that international links imply that it is impossible to control domestic prices by controlling _____ money alone and that _____ money will have to be controlled as well.

8. _____ believe there is no *useful* trade-off between unemployment and inflation.

9. _____ are relatively more concerned with unemployment than with unanticipated inflation.

10. _____ defend the free market and oppose government intervention.

11. The gold standard assumes that the relative price of gold in terms of a representative market basket will be _____.

Self-Test: True–False

1. Proponents of the money growth-rate rule argue it would eliminate recessions.

2. The rational expectations case against countercyclical policy is accepted by most economists.

3. Evidence that showed prices were more flexible than had been believed would support the rational expectations case against countercyclical policy.

4. If foreign and domestic markets are well integrated (that is, currencies of various countries are close substitutes), then what matters is not the quantity of any one country's currency but the world money supply.

5. All economists believe a money growth-rate rule would act as an effective bulwark against tampering with the money stock by special-interest groups.

6. Semi-rules prescribe a particular reaction to a given economic state rather than locking the Fed into a simple growth rate.

7. Monetarists tend to give less weight to cost-push inflation because they look at the price level as a whole. (Price increases in one area should generate price reductions in others.)

8. Economists who believe in rational expectations believe the Fed should pursue a countercyclical policy because the Fed has better information than the public.

9. Some economists think we should define a unit of value as equal to a commodity bundle and then allow the free market to develop any medium of exchange desired. Government's role would be limited to enforcing contracts, checking to see that the parties exchanged goods or services equal in value to the number of commodity bundles specified.

10. According to Friederich von Hayek's private money scheme, private banks would be allowed to produce money if they held government bonds as backing.

Self-Test: Multiple Choice

1. The gold standard does not prevent the Fed from creating inflation if
   a. more gold is discovered.
   b. other countries also create inflation.
   c. full employment requires inflation.
   d. unions demand unreasonable wage increases.
   e. Both a and b.

2. The six beliefs that characterize monetarist theory include only one of the following:
   a. Wage demands are the dominant factor driving income.
   b. Money growth significantly shifts resources between sectors.

c. A complex economy requires a complex set of several equations to describe.

d. The private sector is stable if left alone.

e. Oil price shocks can be a dominant explanation of inflation.

3. While it is true semi-rules outperform rules in simulation studies, these studies are biased against the rule because they do not allow

   a. the lag of policy effectiveness to vary.

   b. for the development of money substitutes.

   c. velocity to vary unpredictably.

   d. higher inflation to boost employment.

   e. Both *a* and *b.*

4. The Fed could increase the money supply faster than the rule allows by

   a. increasing the interest rate.

   b. changing regulators to decrease the liquidity of near-monies.

   c. redefining money to exclude some rapidly growing component.

   d. shifting to a borrowed reserves target.

   e. asking the Treasury to sell more bonds.

5. Under a gold standard, if the Fed increased money growth rapidly

   a. the value of the dollar compared to foreign currencies would rise.

   b. foreigners would be attracted to the dollar by high interest rates.

   c. dollar holders would buy gold, then foreign currency, and finally dollars again, making a profit on the triangular deal.

   d. the Treasury would be forced to buy gold.

   e. our gold reserves would increase.

6. All of the following are characteristic monetarist policy prescriptions *except* that

   a. the Fed should use the money stock rather than the interest rate as the target.

   b. there is a usable inflation-unemployment trade-off.

   c. we need to worry more about unanticipated inflation than about unemployment.

   d. free markets are to be preferred to government intervention.

   e. the instrument of monetary policy should be the base.

7. The OPEC price increase is sometimes used to argue against the money growth-rate rule because

   a. the price increase could lead to a recession that the Fed might want to partially offset.

b. the Fed foolishly increased the money growth rate at the time.

c. inflation could reduce the real price for oil.

d. the episode proved prices are inflexible.

e. the episode sparked a wave of financial innovation that changed the definition of money.

8. An argument against the rule is that
   a. velocity may grow more slowly than expected and this could generate a period of inflation until the inflation is anticipated.
   b. velocity could grow more slowly than expected generating a prolonged recession until wages and prices adjust.
   c. velocity could grow more rapidly than expected and this would cause a prolonged recession until wages and prices adjust.
   d. the Fed's record of procyclical policy is well established.
   e. the Fed should ignore exchange rates when setting monetary policy.

9. The following is an argument against a money growth-rate rule:
   a. Prices are inflexible.
   b. Expectations are rational.
   c. There is political pressure to inflate the money stock.
   d. Our economic knowledge is extremely limited.
   e. The rule of law is better than the rule of man.

10. Friedman claims that only part of the argument for a money growth-rate rule is economic. The other part is
    a. religious.
    b. psychological.
    c. sociological.
    d. political.
    e. scientific.

Topics for Discussion

1. What do you think is the weakest aspect of Friedman's argument for a constant money growth-rate rule? Why?

2. What is Friedman's best argument for a money growth-rate rule? The best counterargument?

3. The text sticks quite carefully to countercyclical monetary policy. What other sort of government economic programs are possible? Are they subject to the same criticisms?

4. If a money growth-rate rule were established, can you think of any changes that could be made and that would help the rule by

making prices more flexible? (Why might prices be inflexible?) Or any changes that would keep the characteristics of money from changing?

Exercise Questions

1*a.* Construct a list of arguments for the money growth-rate rule.

   b. Construct a list of arguments against the money growth-rate rule.

Put an E by each argument that is economic and a P by those that rely on political judgments or values. Those arguments that are economic are potentially resolvable through further research.

2. The following quotes come from a debate between Milton Friedman and Franco Modigliani over stabilization policy.[1] Your task is to identify the speaker. Franco Modigliani is arguing for countercyclical policy while Milton Friedman is supporting the money growth-rate rule.

   a. ". . . monetary policy is an appropriate and proper tool directed at achieving price stability . . . but is not an appropriate tool for achieving a particular target rate of unemployment."

   b. "They [the Fed] can do anything with money, as long as they tell us what their real targets are—and as long as they take the blame when they do not hit the real targets."

   c. "It seemed to me at that time [1974] that everybody who had any common sense would agree . . . that when you get an outside supply shock of the magnitude experienced in that year, you do need to relax your money supply rules and allow for a more rapid growth of the money supply."

   d. "What happened in 1974 was not that the Fed did not accommodate; what happened was that the Fed stepped hard on the brakes . . . We agreed at that time, not precisely on what the right policy was, but what the right direction of policy was."

   e. "My only point is to demonstrate that there is nothing about the price rise from 1971 to 1974 which is not entirely consistent with earlier changes in the quantity of money."

[1] The debate was published in the *Federal Reserve Bank of San Francisco Economic Review* (Spring 1977) Supplement.

f. "The explosion of prices was an explosion, because the rate of inflation of, say the CPI, went up from something like 7 to something like 13 from the second quarter of '73 to the first of '74. And if anybody believes that an explosion of prices of this sort can be accounted for by these wiggles in the money supply, well, he can believe anything."

g. "This sounds just like advising a man in Minneapolis, who wants to go down to New Orleans, along the following lines: 'Look here, there are two ways to go. I know you are trying to go by car; but there is only one way to go that is sure. You should put yourself in a tub and drift down the river. Because we know that the Mississippi River has a current, you can't fail to get there eventually. Whereas, if you take the car, you might make a wrong turn and you might end up in Alaska. You might catch pneumonia. You might never get there.'"

(The following quotes refer to a disagreement about which historical period exhibited the most stable money growth. One discussant believes the 1953–57 period was stable based on deviations from a constant growth while the other believes 1961–65 or –66 was stable. In the 1953–57 period there was a boom followed by a recession while the 1961–66 period was one of steady growth. Again, identify Friedman or Modigliani.)

h. "Is that 1961–65 a stable period? Do you realize that *M-1* went from 1.5 percent up to 7 percent?"

i. "Of course; but they were proceeding along a steady path."

j. ". . . [T]his is the really important insight of the rational-expectations approach, in my opinion . . . a world in which you do not have agreement between the actual and anticipated rate of money change, that model . . . would have been different in a world where you do."

k. "Who looks at the money supply? What merchant, what industry, looks at the money supply?"

l. "Nobody. Who cares whether they look at it?"

m. "Okay; but then what does the expected money supply matter? If I don't look at it, how can I expect it?"

n. ". . . [S]tubbornly insisting on stable money growth is wrong when we have just observed a great decline in the demand for money."

o. "Oh no we haven't."

p. "If you are very careful and distribute the weight properly, you can drive a car with three wheels. Does it follow, however, that I should advise you to do it?"

q. "So what evidence do you really offer that we know enough so that we know how to handle that fourth wheel to be more stable, rather than less stable?"

Answers to Self-Tests

Completion

1. positive; destabilizing
2. rising; fall
3. semi-rule
4. incomes
5. inflexible; stable
6. substitutes
7. domestic; foreign
8. Monetarists
9. Keynesians
10. Monetarists
11. stable

True–False

1. False	6. True
2. False	7. True
3. True	8. False
4. True	9. True
5. False	10. False

Multiple Choice

1. *e*	6. *b*
2. *d*	7. *a*
3. *a*	8. *b*
4. *c*	9. *a*
5. *c*	10. *d*

Answers to Exercise Questions

1*a.* *Sample arguments for a constant money growth-rate rule:*
   Constant money growth would lead to a more stable and more predictable rate of inflation. This is important because the cost

of unanticipated inflation is much higher than the cost of anticipated inflation. (E)

The distributed lag of monetary policy is long and highly variable. Until we are better at predicting both the effect of policy
and the path of the economy, interference is more likely to do
harm than good. (E)

The only legitimate goal of the Fed is the stabilization of
nominal values such as the price level. Real variables are inappropriate goals. (E) However, the Fed is distracted by political
pressures to pursue inappropriate goals like interest-rate stabilization or full employment. (P)

Rational expectations theory suggests that whatever the Fed
does will be adjusted to by the general public. The impact of
policy then depends critically on the interaction of Fed action
and public reaction. The more stable Fed policy is, the more
predictable public reaction will be. (E)

Knowledge that the Fed is pursuing a stable growth-rate rule
will reduce the uncertainty savers and investors face. With less
uncertainty there will be more growth and more stability. (E)

As a general principle, government ought to rely on the rule of
law rather than the rule of authorities. (P)

b. *Arguments against the money growth-rate rule:*

We know enough about the economy and the impact of Fed
policy so that some small attempts at stabilization policy are
appropriate. (E)

The lags are not that long or variable. (E)

While the Fed's record is not good, they can and will do
better. (P)

Wage and price inflexibility negates much of the rational
expectations argument. (E)

Given a supply shock, a constant money growth-rate rule
allows too great a drop in output. (P)

Variations in the demand for money may mean the economy
is less stable with a constant money growth-rate rule. (E)

There may be severe adjustment costs to a constant money
growth rate that is significantly lower than the current money
growth rate. (E)

The rule could be evaded. (P)

Control over the growth rate of one country's money would
be insufficient. (E)

Other goals, like interest-rate stability and full employment,
are legitimate goals of the Fed. (E) The Fed should be free to
pursue policies that trade off the competing goals. (P)

A rule would be abandoned as soon as following the rule
became politically burdensome. (P)

2a. Friedman
 b. Modigliani
 c. Modigliani
 d. Friedman
 e. Friedman
 f. Modigliani
 g. Modigliani
 h. Modigliani
 i. Friedman
 j. Friedman
 k. Modigliani
 l. Friedman
 m. Modigliani
 n. Modigliani
 o. Friedman
 p. Modigliani
 q. Friedman

CHAPTER 26   The Evolution of the International Monetary System

Learning Objectives

After studying this chapter, you should be able to

1. describe the three international monetary systems of the last century.

2. cite the advantages and disadvantages of each system.

3. discuss the factors which caused one system to give way in favor of the next one.

Key Terms, Concepts, and Institutions

You should be able to define or explain

gold standard
gold-exchange standard
Bretton Woods system
bimetallic standard
pegged exchange rates
limping gold standard
bills of exchange
International Bank for
  Reconstruction and Development (IBRD or World Bank)

Internaional Trade
  Organization (ITO)
GATT (General Agreement on
  Tariffs and Trade)
International Monetary Fund
  (IMF)
SDRs (Special Drawing Rights)
floating exchange rate
Smithsonian Agreement

Self-Test: Completion

1. An alternative to shipping gold which lowered shipping and insurance costs was to ship _____ .

2. A country which shipped gold to settle a balance-of-payments deficit (increased/decreased) its money supply and (increased/decreased) its national price level.

3. The _____ standard developed as a result of an anticipated shortage of gold in the 1920s.

4. Under the gold-exchange standard, the two countries which did not have to ship gold in response to balance-of-payments deficits

   were _____ and _____.

5. The _____ makes loans to countries to help them get through temporary foreign-exchange difficulties.

6. The _____ is a Bretton Woods institution created to facilitate the postwar reconstruction in Europe, and which now extends financial assistance to developing countries.

7. The dominant agency which promotes tariff reductions

   and removal of other trade barriers is the _____.

8. The IMF issues _____, an international asset consisting of a market basket of the major currencies.

9. The _____ of 1972 resulted in the devaluation of the U.S. dollar.

10. The current international monetary system is _____.

Self-Test: True–False

1. The gold standard came about as a result of international agreements.

2. Adherence to the gold standard resulted in pegged exchange rates.

3. Under the gold standard, gold would flow out of a country, which incurred a balance-of-payments deficit.

4. Countries under the gold standard had complete control of their money supplies.

5. The advantage of the gold standard was the potential for stable commodity prices in the long run.

6. The IMF lends money to member countries without exacting any conditions from them as to how they intend to run their economic policies.

7. The value of Special Drawing Rights is specified by the IMF in terms of gold.

8. The U.S. balance-of-payments deficits from 1950 to the mid-1960s resulted from a decline in the competitiveness of U.S. manufactured goods.

9. Countries on a limping gold standard increased the price of gold whenever the demand for gold increased.

10. A country whose imports exceed its exports has a balance-of-trade surplus.

Self-Test: Multiple Choice

1. U.S. balance-of-payments deficits from 1950 to the mid-1960s were primarily the result of
   a. the desire of other countries to add to their dollar holdings.
   b. an increase in petroleum imports.
   c. loss of the competitive edge by U.S. manufacturers.
   d. a high U.S. inflation rate relative to the inflation rate of its major trading partners.
   e. All of the above.

2. Today most of the major trading countries are on a
   a. gold-exchange standard.
   b. gold standard.
   c. limping gold standard.
   d. floating exchange-rate system.
   e. bimetallic system.

3. If the exchange rate of francs in terms of dollars is FF1 = $.193, then the exchange rate of dollars in terms of francs is
   a. FF 107.1.
   b. FF 5.18.
   c. FF .0093.
   d. $1.07.1.
   e. $5.18.

4. Under the gold standard, if the official price of gold increased, market forces would cause
   a. the money supply to increase and the price level to fall.
   b. the money stock to increase and the price level to rise.
   c. the money stock to decrease and the price level to fall.
   d. the money stock to decrease and the price level to rise.
   e. no change in the money supply or prices.

5. Under the gold standard, exchange rates
   a. were fixed.
   b. were flexible within narrow limits.
   c. were fixed by central banks.
   d. were completely flexible.
   e. None of the above.

6. Under flexible exchange rates, an increase in U.S. imports of Japanese cars would cause
   a. the dollar to rise against the yen.
   b. the yen to rise against the dollar.
   c. gold to flow into the U.S.
   d. gold to flow out of the U.S.
   e. a and c.

7. Under the "rules of the game" of the gold standard
   a. countries with balance-of-payments deficits would increase their money stocks.
   b. countries with balance-of-payments deficits would decrease their money stocks.
   c. countries with balance-of-payments surpluses would increase their money stocks.
   d. countries with balance-of-payments surpluses would decrease their money stocks.
   e. b and c.

8. Under the gold standard, if the supply of gold increased rapidly due to new gold discoveries in South Africa
   a. the general price level would rise for all countries on the gold standard.
   b. the general price level would rise in South Africa.
   c. the general price level would fall for all countries on the gold standard.
   d. the general price level would fall in South Africa.
   e. the price level would not change.

9. A country experiencing balance-of-payments problems would apply for a loan to
   a. the World Bank.
   b. the ITO.
   c. the IMF.
   d. the IBRD.
   e. a and c.

10. The Bretton Woods system
    a. established the IMF.
    b. established the World Bank.

c. was the result of an international treaty.

d. was established under the premise that there would be a perpetual dollar shortage.

e. All of the above.

Topics for Discussion

1. Some critics suggest that the United States could attain price stability if only it would return to the gold standard. What would have to be done for the United States to return to the gold standard? Would this guarantee stable prices?

2. Explain how the *expectation* of a devaluation could cause the devaluation to occur under fixed exchange rates.

3. It has been said that the Bretton Woods system creates a restrictive policy bias for nations with chronic balance-of-payments deficits. Explain how this could be true.

4. Compare and contrast the functions of the IBRD and the IMF.

5. Discuss the advantages and disadvantages of fixed versus flexible exchange rates.

Exercise Questions

1. The *Wall Street Journal* of September 13, 1983, reported that Zaire had decided to float its currency, the Zaire. The Zaire was pegged to the IMF's Special Drawing Rights since 1967. The Zaire had been devalued from a rate comparable to 6.06 per U.S. dollar to 29.9 per U.S. dollar.

   a. Bankers and diplomats praised Zaire's decision to devalue. What major group will benefit from this devaluation?

   b. The decision to devalue was a blow to black marketers in Zaire. Why? (What had they been doing?)

2. The following report is from the *Wall Street Journal*, September 13, 1983: "Brazil has promised to sign by Thursday the letter of intent that is expected to release new credits from the International Monetary Fund. . . . Details of Brazil's letter of intent to the IMF weren't disclosed, but the document is supposed to lay out Brazil's promises through 1984 for curbing inflation and restoring more order to its financial house. . . ."

a. Brazil applied to the IMF and not the World Bank. What does it need the loans for?

b. How does the IMF justify intervening in Brazil's internal affairs by requiring it to lay out proposals for curbing inflation, etc.?

3. If the U.S. dollar will buy 151 Mexican pesos, how many dollars will a Mexican peso buy?

Answers to Self-Tests

Completion

1. bills of exchange
2. decreased; decreased
3. gold exchange
4. Great Britain; United States
5. International Monetary Fund (IMF)
6. International Bank for Reconstruction and Development (IBRD, or World Bank)
7. GATT (General Agreement on Tariffs and Trade)
8. SDRs (Special Drawing Rights)
9. Smithsonian Agreement
10. floating exchange rates

True–False

1. False	6. False
2. True	7. False
3. True	8. False
4. False	9. True
5. True	10. False

Multiple Choice

1. *a*	6. *b*
2. *d*	7. *e*
3. *b*	8. *a*
4. *b*	9. *c*
5. *b*	10. *e*

Answers to Exercise Questions

1a. Exporters. Their goods will be cheaper now in terms of other countries.

b. It wiped out the gap between the official and black market rates for Zaires, and wiped out the opportunity to profit by this differential.

2a. The fact that Brazil applied to the IMF and not to the World Bank indicates that the loans are to cover short-term balance-of-payments problems as opposed to long-term capital financing projects.

b. The IMF takes the view that credit should be extended only if there is a reasonable prospect that the member country can resolve its balance-of-payments problems.

3. $1 = 151 pesos
$1/151 pesos = 151 pesos/151 pesos
$.0066666/pesos = 1
$.0066225 = 1 peso.

CHAPTER 27   The Organization of the Foreign Exchange Market

Learning Objectives

After studying this chapter, you should be able to

1. understand the major forces behind the supply and demand for one currency versus supply and demand for another.

2. explain how institutions actually conduct the exchange of one currency for another.

3. explain why the purchasing-power-parity theory helps explain the changes in the relative values of currencies.

4. show the interrelationships between the spot and forward rates between two currencies and the two countries' interest rates.

5. understand how the expected spot rate and the forward rate for any currency are related.

6. understand how importers and exporters can use the forward-exchange markets to reduce risk.

7. read the balance-of-payments accounts.

Key Terms, Concepts, and Institutions

You should be able to define or explain

exchange rate
balance of payments
fixed vs. floating exchange rates
bid-ask spread
spot-exchange rate

speculators
arbitragers
purchasing-power-parity theory
Fisher proposition
intervention

forward-exchange rate   current account
interest-rate-parity theorem capital account

Self-Test: Completion

1. If someone contracts today to trade marks for dollars at an agreed-upon price in thirty days they have sold marks _____.

2. If someone agrees to deliver marks in two days at an agreed-upon price they have used the _____ market.

3. If a bank has more mark-denominated assets than liabilities then they have taken a _____ position in marks.

4. If the inflation rate in the U.S. is lower than the rate in Germany then the mark/dollar exchange rate will tend to _____ according to the _____ theorem.

5. If the interest rates in Germany increased then the forward premium of the mark would tend to _____ according to the _____ theorem.

6. If people expect the spot-exchange rate will rise in the future then the current spot-exchange rate will tend to _____.

7. Someone who uses his unusually low transaction costs to buy some currency where its price is low and sell it where its price is high, or uses the forward- and spot-exchange markets plus the capital markets to make an instantaneous riskless profit, is a(n) _____.

8. Someone who makes money by correctly guessing how spot- or forward-exchange rates will change is a(n) _____.

9. If the U.S. stock market has a record boom, the foreign purchase of U.S. assets will tend to _____ the value of the dollar.

10. If the foreign tourists buy U.S. goods by using travelers checks drawn against their hometown bank this would increase the _____ account, reduce the _____ account, and tend to _____ the value of the dollar.

11. Through the summer of 1986 the dollar was falling partly in response to rapid money growth here. Paul Volcker wanted other countries to help slow the dollar's slide. He asked them to

_____ their interest rates.

Self-Test: True–False

1. Transaction costs for forward-exchange rates are higher for more volatile currencies.

2. A U.S. importer of Japanese cars could get the yen he will need by selling yen forward.

3. Most exchanges between foreign currencies and the dollar occur within the U.S.

4. If you know you will need marks in the future, you could buy marks now and invest in Germany, or you could invest in the U.S. and buy marks forward.

5. If you believe the spot mark/dollar rate will be 2 in ninety days, and the currently quoted ninety-day future rate is 3, then you believe it would be profitable to sell marks forward and meet the contractual obligation by buying marks at the spot rate in ninety days.

6. Exchange rates have been more variable than the purchasing-power-parity theory would seem to indicate.

7. Currencies are very nearly perfect substitutes for each other because there is little uncertainty in foreign-exchange markets.

8. It has been demonstrated that those who use the forward-exchange markets to reduce risk pay a heavy risk premium.

9. If a currency is more expensive in the forward- than spot-exchange markets then it is at a forward discount.

10. According to the purchasing-power-parity theory, if the rate of inflation of tradeable goods is 5 percent higher in the U.S. than in Germany, then the mark/dollar rate should decline 5 percent a year.

1. If the forward premium on marks is larger than the difference between U.S. and German interest rates then it would be more profitable to
   a. invest in the U.S. than in Germany.
   b. invest in Germany rather than the U.S.
   c. borrow in Germany rather than the U.S.
   d. sell marks forward and acquire the marks you will need in the spot-exchange market thirty days from now.
   e. buy marks forward and sell them in the spot-exchange market in thirty days.

2. If you know you will receive marks in the future and you want to insulate yourself from exchange-rate risk you can
   a. sell dollars forward.
   b. buy marks forward.
   c. sell marks forward.
   d. sell marks spot.
   e. take out an insurance policy with the Chicago Mercantile Exchange.

3. If the mark/dollar rate is 2.6 and the yen/dollar rate is 243, then the yen/mark rate must be
   a. 631.8.
   b. .236.
   c. 48.6.
   d. .0107.
   e. 93.5.

4. The bid-ask spread
   a. is larger in big city banks than in smaller banks.
   b. first states the exchange rate used when buying marks from customers and then states the exchange rate used when providing customers with marks.
   c. is set by a cartel.
   d. tends to be larger for more stable currencies.
   e. is at least equal to 1 percent of the dollar value of the transaction.

5. The forward-exchange rate is likely to be an unbiased predictor of the future spot-exchange rate because
   a. the willingness of each group of importers to pay a risk premium tends to be offsetting.
   b. it is estimated by skilled economists.
   c. on average the actual mark/dollar spot-exchange rate is below the rate predicted by the forward-exchange market.

     d. the uncertainty of foreign exchange demands a risk premium.

     e. exchange rates are stable enough so that it is easy to make accurate predictions.

6. The purchasing-power-parity theory

     a. is a theory of social justice.

     b. states that tradeable goods in different countries should have the same price after an allowance is made for transportation costs and the exchange rate.

     c. is a relationship between the forward premium or discount and interest rates.

     d. depends critically on what people expect the spot-exchange rate will be in the future.

     e. quite accurately predicts short-term movements in exchange rates.

7. The Fisher proposition

     a. depends on arbitragers.

     b. is a relationship linking the inflation rates of two countries.

     c. depends on speculators to bet on their guesses about the future spot-exchange rates of some currency.

     d. states that if the interest rate in the U.S. is higher than the interest rate in Germany then speculators believe the mark/dollar rate will increase.

     e. is identical to the interest-rate-parity theorem.

8. A central bank could intervene in the foreign-exchange markets

     a. to keep their currency from appreciating by buying their own currency with foreign-exchange reserves.

     b. to keep their currency from depreciating by selling their own currency and building up foreign-exchange reserves.

     c. to encourage currency appreciation by reducing the domestic money stock leading to a higher interest rate.

     d. to encourage currency depreciation by reducing inflation.

     e. to encourage exports by buying their own currency.

9. Central bank intervention

     a. is currently required of the U.S. to maintain a stated dollar/gold exchange rate.

     b. is much less frequent than it used to be under the Bretton Woods system.

     c. depends on the size of foreign-exchange reserves which central banks have or are willing to maintain.

     d. rarely conflicts with domestic monetary policy.

     e. always changes the domestic money supply.

10. Domestic monetary policy is likely to have larger domestic and smaller foreign effects if
    a. exchange rates are fixed.
    b. currencies are good substitutes for each other.
    c. tariff barriers are removed.
    d. exchange rates fluctuate unpredictably.
    e. All but d.

Topics for Discussion

1. What are the major advantages of a fixed exchange-rate system?

2. What are the major advantages of a flexible exchange-rate system?

3. Does the presence of a forward-exchange market for periods up to a year mean importers and exporters face no foreign-exchange-rate risk?

4. Why is the Fisher proposition likely to be a better guide when exchange rates are relatively stable?

5. Purchasing-power parity depends on actual trade of physical goods. What sort of price index would fit the theory best?

6. Is purchasing-power parity likely to be a better predictor of exchange rates in the short run or the long run? Why?

7. On October 1, 1986, the *Wall Street Journal* reported that the West German central bank was buying dollars. Volcker continued his plea for lower German interest rates to achieve the same end. What difference does it make whether the German central bank boosts the dollar by direct purchases or by reducing their interest rates?

8. The *Wall Street Journal* article titled "U.S. Treasury Debt Is Increasingly Traded Globally and Nonstop"[1] reported that the international trading of U.S. government debt has been spurred by the huge U.S. deficit, deregulation of financial markets abroad, and U.S. regulations allowing foreign investors to buy government securities tax free. Why do we give foreign investors a tax break? How does this affect the dollar value? Our exports? Which industries and governments benefit from the flow of capital from abroad to the U.S.? Which lose?

[1] *Wall Street Journal*, September 10, 1986, p. 1.

Exercise Questions

1. Calculate the price in pounds of a Chevette selling for $10,000 given the following exchange rates:

   pounds/dollar = .75   pound price (*a:* _____)

   pounds/dollar = 1.0   pound price (*b:* _____)

   Given these calculations, we expect the quantity of Chevettes sold in Britain to (*c:* increase/decrease) as the pound price of the dollar rises. This helps explain why the (*d:* demand for/supply of) dollars is (*e:* upward/downward) sloping.
       Calculate the price in dollars of an M.G.B. midget whose pound sterling price is 7,500 given the exchange rates below:

   pounds/dollar = .75   dollar price (*f:* _____)

   pounds/dollar = 1.0   dollar price (*g:* _____)

   Given these calculations, we expect the quantity of midgets sold in the U.S. to (*h:* increase/decrease) as the pound price of the dollar rises. This helps explain why the (*i:* demand/supply) of dollars is (*j:* upward/downward) sloping.

2. An increase in the U.S. interest rates will (*a:* increase/decrease) the demand for dollars as more people with pounds choose to buy U.S. rather than U.K. securities. Similarly, the higher U.S. interest rates will (*b:* increase/decrease) the supply of dollars as more people with dollars choose to buy U.S. securities. These two effects lead to a (*c:* higher/lower) pound/dollar exchange rate. This is a(n) (*d:* appreciation/depreciation) of the dollar.
       An increase in the U.S. rate of inflation would (*e:* increase/decrease) the supply of dollars as people with dollars try to buy more U.K. goods and would (*f:* increase/decrease) the demand for dollars as people with pounds buy fewer U.S. goods. These two effects lead to a (*g:* higher/lower) pound/dollar exchange rate. This is a(n) (*h:* appreciation/depreciation) of the dollar.

3. The following spot- and forward-exchange rates for August 23, 1983, are quoted from the August 24 issue of the *Wall Street Journal*:

pound/dollar spot-exchange rate	.6555
pound/dollar 180-day forward-exchange rate	.6539

   The dollar is selling at an annual percentage forward

   (*a:* premium/discount) of (*b:* _____) percent. The market believes the dollar will (*c:* appreciate/depreciate) against the pound.

According to the interest-rate-parity theory the interest rate in the U.S. should have been (*d:* _____) percent (*e:* above/ below) the interest rate in the U.K. on freely traded securities of equal risk and transaction costs.

If in 180 days the pound/dollar rate is .7 then it would be profitable to sell 100,000 pounds forward for (*f:* _____) dollars only to buy the 100,000 pounds at the spot-exchange rate in 180 days for (*g:* $_____) and a profit of (*h:* $_____). Therefore if people expect that the pound/dollar rate in 180 days will be .7, they will sell pounds forward until the pound/dollar forward rate equals .7.

Answers to Self-Tests

Completion

1. forward
2. spot
3. long
4. rise; purchasing-power-parity
5. decline; interest-rate-parity
6. rise
7. arbitrager
8. speculator
9. increase
10. current; capital; increase
11. decrease

True–False

1. True	6. True
2. False	7. False
3. False	8. False
4. True	9. False
5. False	10. True

Multiple Choice

1. *b*	6. *b*
2. *c*	7. *c*
3. *e*	8. *c*
4. *b*	9. *c*
5. *a*	10. *d*

Answers to Exercise Questions

1a. 7,500
 b. 10,000
 c. decrease
 d. demand for
 e. downward
 f. 10,000
 g. 7,500
 h. increase
 i. supply
 j. upward

2a. increase
 b. decrease
 c. higher
 d. appreciation
 e. increase
 f. decrease
 g. lower
 h. depreciation

3a. discount
 b. 1/2
 c. depreciate
 d. 1/2
 e. above
 f. 152,929
 g. 142,857
 h. 10,072

CHAPTER 28 International Banking and National Monetary Policies

Learning Objectives

After studying this chapter, you should be able to

1. describe the changes in the international banking system since 1960.

2. understand the concept of offshore markets and explain why offshore banks have a regulatory advantage over domestic banks.

3. explain the two opposing theories of credit creation in the offshore markets and the implications for the growth of the world inflation rate.

4. explain how the growth of offshore markets weakens the effectiveness of national monetary policies.

5. cite policies which the Federal Reserve might adopt to discourage the growth of offshore markets and reduce the regulatory advantages enjoyed by offshore banks.

Key Terms, Concepts, and Institutions

You should be able to define or explain

external currency market
Eurodollar market
offshore banking market
monetary havens
reciprocity in banking
Edge Act

the principle of national
treatment
International Banking Facilities
(IBFs)
International Banking Act of
1978 (IBA)

Self-Test: Completion

1. _____ are dollar-denominated deposits issued by a banking office ouside the United States.

2. U.S. banks are (larger/smaller) and (more/less) numerous than foreign banks.

3. Offshore deposits increase when interest rates (rise/fall).

4. The _____ Act reduced the regulatory advantages enjoyed by foreign banks in the United States.

5. If the offshore market is exclusively an interbank market, it (does/does not) have a significant impact on the world inflation rate.

6. The growth of offshore deposits (raises/lowers) a bank's effective reserve requirement and (increases/decreases) the money multiplier.

7. _____ can issue deposits not subject to reserve requirements.

8. U.S. investors have an incentive to hold offshore deposits as long as U.S. reserve requirements are (higher/lower) than elsewhere.

9. The _____ market sells deposits and makes loans denominated in a currency other than that of the country in which they are located.

10. The banking industries of the major countries are (more/less) concentrated than the banking industry in the U.S.

Self-Test: True–False

1. Offshore banks generally offer higher interest rates on deposits than do domestic banks.

2. The internationalization of commercial banking has decreased competition in the major international centers as banks move to other markets.

3. The growth of the offshore market has enhanced the effectiveness of national monetary policies.

4. Both foreign and U.S. banks expanded overseas in order to circumvent domestic limits on growth.

5. Foreign banks involved in retail banking must subscribe to FDIC insurance.

6. The national treatment principle has priority over the reciprocity principle.

7. The assessment of the risk associated with offshore deposits has increased in the last decade.

8. The United States could reduce the incentive for investors to hold offshore deposits by raising the reserve requirements for domestic banks.

9. The Fed permitted banks to establish IBFs in 1980.

10. Interest rates differ between domestic banks and offshore banks, but all offshore banks offer the same interest rates on deposits.

Self-Test: Multiple Choice

1. The internationalization of commercial banking has resulted in
   a. a drain of dollars from the United States to Europe.
   b. a higher world inflation rate.
   c. increased competition in the major international financial centers.
   d. unstable exchange rates.
   e. All of the above.

2. Euromarks
   a. are dollar-denominated deposits issued by a banking office located in Germany.
   b. are deposits denominated in marks issued by a banking office located outside of Germany.
   c. are mark-denominated deposits issued by banking offices located in Germany.
   d. constitute 10 percent of the offshore deposits issued by banks in Western Europe.
   e. are attractive to investors because the rate they must pay on deposits is lower than that of domestic banks.

3. Offshore banks
   a. can offer higher interest rates on deposits than domestic banks can.
   b. are generally not subject to reserve requirements.
   c. are generally not subject to interest-rate ceilings.
   d. are usually branches or subsidiaries of major international banks.
   e. All of the above.

4. A foreign branch of a U.S. bank
   a. is legally incorporated in the country in which it is located.
   b. is taxed on its income when dividends are paid to the parent bank.
   c. cannot fail as long as the parent bank is operating.
   d. All of the above.
   e. a and c.

5. U.S. banks expanded abroad
   a. to follow their U.S. clients.
   b. to avoid domestic limits on growth.
   c. to participate in the offshore money market.
   d. to avoid losing deposits to foreign banks which could offer higher rates of interest on deposits.
   e. All of the above.

6. Foreign banks in the U.S.
   a. must buy FDIC insurance if they engage in retail banking.
   b. must join the Fed.
   c. are restricted from setting up Edge Act corporations.
   d. are subject to the regulations of their country of origin under the national treatment principle.
   e. are subject to the same regulations as U.S. banks in their country of origin under the reciprocity principle.

7. There has been concern about the rapid growth of offshore deposits *mainly* because
   a. there is empirical evidence which suggests that the growth of offshore deposits increases the world inflation rate.
   b. offshore banks are extremely unstable and prone to collapse because they do not keep reserves against deposits.
   c. the growth of offshore deposits adversely affects exchange rates.
   d. the effectiveness of national monetary policies is reduced.
   e. All of the above.

8. The growth of offshore deposits
   a. is mainly the result of the surge in the world inflation rate.
   b. accelerates when interest rates rise.
   c. offers investors a risk-free alternative to domestic deposits.
   d. will accelerate if exchange controls are adopted.
   e. All of the above.

9. The expansion of foreign banks into the United States in the 1970s occurred for all of the following reasons *except* that
   a. they wished to participate in the financing of international trade between their home country and the U.S.
   b. they wished to serve ethnic markets in the U.S.

c. they followed their clients overseas.
  d. they wanted to avoid nationalization in their home countries.
  e. they wanted to circumvent domestic restrictions on growth.
10. Select the false statement(s):
  a. Investors perceive additional risks with offshore deposits that they do not face with domestic deposits.
  b. Banks are forbidden to use offshore deposits to finance domestic loans.
  c. Banks have the ability to charge loan customers lower rates on offshore loans because their costs are lower.
  d. Country of domicile of the parent bank affects investors' risk perceptions of offshore banks.
  e. The structure of U.S. financial regulation cannot be independent of regulations made elsewhere.

Topics for Discussion

1. Virtually all Eurodollar deposits are time deposits. How does this fact enter into the discussion about whether Eurodollars ought to be included in the U.S. money supply?

2. In what phase of the business cycle are offshore banks most likely to be involved in circumventing national monetary policies? Why?

3. Should Eurodollar markets be regulated? Why or why not? If you feel that they should be regulated, who should do the regulating?

4. What is meant by the internationalization of the commercial banking system? What factors help speed this process?

Exercise Questions

1. Some analysts argue that the existence of the Eurodollar market encourages speculation in currencies. Suppose you think that the value of the dollar is going to decline relative to the yen in the near future. If you were a currency speculator, what transactions might you undertake in the Eurodollar market? What would happen to the value of the dollar relative to the yen if everyone reacted as you did?

2. The following report appeared in the *Wall Street Journal*, September 22, 1983: "Singapore plans to offer tax breaks to offshore funds in an effort to lure foreign investors and financial institu-

tions away from Hong Kong." Suppose the U.S. approaches Singapore about regulating offshore banks, perhaps asking Singapore to force them to hold reserves against deposits. How do you think Singapore will respond?

Answers to Self-Tests

Completion

1. Eurodollars
2. larger; more
3. rise
4. International Banking
5. does not
6. lowers; increases
7. IBFs (International Banking Facilities)
8. higher
9. offshore, or external currency
10. more

True–False

1. True	6. True
2. False	7. False
3. False	8. False
4. True	9. True
5. True	10. False

Multiple Choice

1. *c*	7. *d*
2. *b*	8. *b*
3. *e*	9. *d*
4. *c*	10. *b* and *c* are both false
5. *e*	statements
6. *a*	

Answers to Exercise Questions

1. You would borrow in the Eurodollar market to buy Japanese yen, expecting to be able to repay your debt by using your yen to buy dollars after the price of the dollar has fallen. If everyone felt as you did, they'd flood the market with dollars and the value of the dollar would fall.

2. Singapore is likely to lend a deaf ear to U.S. proposals to regulate offshore banking. It is interested in attracting offshore banking, and increased regulation would deter potential entrants.

CHAPTER 29   The Agenda of International Financial Issues

Learning Objectives

After studying this chapter, you should be able to

1. understand why fixed exchange rates aid trade but constrain monetary policy.

2. understand why regions with a single labor market and capital mobility may find it to their advantage to have a single currency.

3. explain why a new international economic order will be difficult to establish.

4. state the historical landmarks in international finance.

5. show why independent monetary policy is not only associated with exchange-rate uncertainty but requires exchange-rate uncertainty.

6. list the relative merits of gold and the dollar as the international reserve asset.

7. argue for and against an international agency that would regulate the stock of reserve assets.

Key Terms, Concepts, and Institutions

You should be able to define or explain

international monetary system   floating exchange rates
monetary independence   destabilizing speculation
pegged exchange rates   efficient market
cosmopolitan interest   crawling peg
optimal currency area   passive borrowing

labor market
segmented markets
political unification

seigniorage
offsetting devaluations
reserve assets

Self-Test: Completion

1. If one country devalues its currency and a trading partner does the same to avoid a change in the exchange rate, then these are

   _____ .

2. The primary motive for currency unification seems to be

   _____ .

3. National governments are likely to press for their own self-interests and may ignore the international or _____ interest.

4. If it is possible to have different interest rates on similar securities in two different countries, then the capital markets are

   said to be _____ .

5. It is sometimes argued that the speculative sale of a currency can lead to its devaluation which in turn will generate inflation since imports will be more expensive. The inflation justifies the currency devaluation. This is an example of _____ speculation.

6. If countries routinely adjust the pegged exchange rates several times a year the scheme is called a _____ peg.

7. In the last few years analysts have used evidence that future exchange-rate changes can be predicted from past exchange-rate changes to argue that the foreign-exchange market is not

   _____ .

8. More expansive monetary policy would tend to lower interest rates and increase expected inflation. Both effects cause the

   currency to _____ .

9. As long as foreign governments were willing to hold more dollars as reserves, the U.S. was able to finance payments deficits

   through _____ .

10. By being the international banker the U.S. earns a profit from

    the production of money called _____ .

11. One of the major advantages of an institution creating international reserves is that reserves could be _____.

Self-Test: True–False

1. Any new international financial arrangements would have to be consistent with the distribution of political and economic power.
2. The Bretton Woods system broke down in 1971 because of an undervalued dollar and because the inflation rates in other countries were too high.
3. Inflation rates have been higher since the demise of the Bretton Woods system.
4. An advantage of the crawling-peg system over a fixed-rate system is that it would reduce speculation on exchange-rate changes.
5. Currency unification will be less costly if the capital market for the region is segmented.
6. If changes in monetary policy lead to rapid fluctuations in expected inflation, then the spot-exchange rate will fluctuate rapidly even if the actual inflation rate is fairly stable.
7. As a practical matter, the best time to switch to a system of fixed exchange rates is whenever the differences between inflation rates are large.
8. The floating-rate system has generated more stable exchange rates than had been anticipated.
9. One of the arguments for a fixed exchange-rate system is that it leads to more segmented capital markets and increases the independence of monetary policy.
10. The uncertainty of flexible rates increases the segmentation of capital markets.

Self-Test: Multiple Choice

1. Currency unification is more likely to be beneficial if
   a. labor markets are segmented.
   b. the merging countries are already quite large.
   c. the business cycles in the countries are similar in timing and amplitude.
   d. before unification different interest rates on similar securities were common.
   e. the countries each have their own language.

2. New international financial arrangements
   a. may have virtually no cost if the treaties merely describe present practices.
   b. are less likely to involve a strong central authority if nationalist pressures become stronger.
   c. would have to give special status to the U.S., Europe, and Japan to be viable.
   d. could offer a forum to coordinate national economic policies.
   e. All of the above.

3. The interwar experience with floating exchange rates led to the belief that
   a. speculation tends to be stabilizing.
   b. floating rates disrupt trade and investment.
   c. floating rates reduce monetary independence.
   d. the interwar inflation was caused by floating rates.
   e. None of the above.

4. The uncertainty of floating exchange rates
   a. disrupts trade but differentiates national currencies and allows for independent monetary policy.
   b. disrupts trade and has no offsetting benefits.
   c. can be perfectly hedged through the use of forward-exchange contracts and therefore imposes no costs.
   d. has a greater impact on large, self-sufficient economies.
   e. means the forward-exchange rate will be a biased predictor of the future spot-exchange rate.

5. One of the problems of managing a pegged-rate system is
   a. changes in parity tend to occur before they are needed.
   b. countries must be willing to pay the domestic political cost of keeping the inflation rates in different countries close to each other.
   c. no one pays much attention when parities are changed.
   d. providing reserves to countries with payments deficits.
   e. Only b and d.

6. Reserve assets
   a. declined alarmingly in the 1970s.
   b. consist entirely of gold.
   c. could only be created in the 1960s if the U.S. ran payments deficits.
   d. probably helped reduce world inflation in the 1970s.
   e. have been kept on a stable growth path by the IMF.

7. The use of the dollar as a reserve asset
   a. has increased despite the demise of the Bretton Woods system.

b. exposes the U.S. to risk since these dollars could be dumped in exchange for another currency.

c. is due to the extensive trade and financial links the U.S. has with the rest of the world.

d. would decline if foreigners lost faith in the ability or resolve of the Fed to control inflation.

e. All of the above.

8. A return to a system of fixed exchange rates would be aided most by

a. rising nationalism.

b. a wide range of emerging economic powers.

c. segmented labor markets.

d. similar rates of inflation among the large trading partners.

e. the invention of a manageable reserve asset.

9. Stop-go monetary policies are likely to lead to

a. more variable exchange rates than the purchasing-power-parity theory would suggest because the spot price is affected by both the present and expected future values of a currency.

b. less variable exchange rates than the purchasing-power-parity theory would suggest.

c. more variable exchange rates because if people suddenly expect more inflation in the U.S. they will acquire dollars before prices rise.

d. more variable exchange rates because a lower interest rate would lead people to acquire more dollars.

e. a return to a fixed exchange-rate system.

Topics for Discussion

1. Would the U.S. and Mexico be good candidates for currency unification? How about England and Ireland?

2. Do you think fixed exchange rates help reduce inflation or would countries simply abandon fixed rates whenever internal and external goals came into conflict?

3. Robert Mundell of Columbia University believes the argument for flexible exchange rates is severely weakened by the fact that currency regions are political rather than economic. His argument begins with a hypothetical situation. Suppose the U.S. and Canada are discussing whether or not to peg exchange rates. In the eastern half of both countries there is inflation associated with the rapid growth in automobile production. In the western

half of both countries there is a recession due to the slow-moving forest products industry. Consider why Mundell would conclude that the case for flexible rates is logically strong only if currencies are regional rather than national.[1]

4. Is the current account likely to be in surplus or deficit for less developed countries? Is this because they are borrowing in order to grow or because they cannot produce enough goods and services?

5. What are the disadvantages of gold as a reserve asset? The dollar?

6. Why do flexible exchange rates lead to segmented capital markets?

Exercise Questions

1. Purchasing-power parity requires that the price level in the U.S. equal the price level in England once the difference in exchange rates is accounted for. The relative form of the purchasing-power-parity theory states that the inflation rate in the U.S. plus the percentage appreciation of the dollar will equal the inflation rate in Britain. This relationship works reasonably well in the long run but not the short run.

In the long run, then, if the inflation rate in the U.S. is 10 percent and the inflation rate in Britain is 7 percent then we would expect a(n) (*a:* appreciation/depreciation) of the dollar of

(*b:* _____) percent. This means dollars should sell at a forward (*c:* premium/discount) of (*d:* _____) percent.

Under a fixed exchange-rate system, the pound price of the dollar would (*e:* appreciate/depreciate/not change). In order to maintain this exchange rate the inflation rate in the U.S. must be (*f:* greater than/equal to/less than) the inflation rate in Britain. This implies that the monetary policies of both countries (*g:* are independent/must be coordinated).

Under a fixed exchange-rate system, then the dollar would sell at a forward (*h:* premium/discount/neither) of (*i:* _____) percent. Given the interest-rate-parity theorem the interest rate in the U.S. would be (*j:* greater than/less than/equal to) the interest rate in Britain. Any attempt by the Fed to increase the interest rate would (*k:* succeed/fail) since money would flow

[1] Mundell's argument is set out in his book, *International Economics*, Macmillan, 1968, pp. 179-181.

from (*l:* the U.S. to the U.K./the U.K. to the U.S.). Therefore fixed rates (*m:* increase/reduce) capital mobility and (*n:* increase/reduce) the effectiveness of monetary policy.

2. During the last few years of the Bretton Woods system the inflation rate in the U.S. was (*a:* higher/lower) than in Germany and Japan. This led to (*b:* more/fewer) U.S. exports and (*c:* more/fewer) U.S. imports. This meant that the dollar reserves held by Germany and Japan (*d:* rose/fell). At the end of the Bretton Woods system the dollar (*e:* appreciated/depreciated) and the value of these dollar holdings (*f:* increased/decreased). To the surprise of many, foreign official holdings of dollars (*g:* increased/decreased). This may have been done to reduce the (*h:* appreciation/depreciation) of the foreign currencies. Such an exchange rate change would have meant that the foreign goods cost (*i:* more/less) in terms of the dollar and U.S. goods cost (*j:* more/less) in terms of their currency. Therefore they would have exported (*k:* more/less) and imported (*l:* more/less), leading to (*m:* more/less) employment in their own country.

Answers to Self-Tests

Completion

1. offsetting devaluations
2. political unification
3. cosmopolitan
4. segmented
5. destabilizing
6. crawling
7. efficient
8. depreciate
9. passive borrowing
10. seigniorage
11. managed

True–False

1. True	6. True
2. False	7. False
3. True	8. False
4. True	9. False
5. False	10. True

Multiple Choice

1. *c*   6. *c*
2. *e*   7. *e*
3. *b*   8. *d*
4. *a*   9. *a*
5. *e*

Answers to Exercise Questions

1*a.* depreciation
  b. 3
  c. discount
  d. 3
  e. not change
  f. equal to
  g. must be coordinated
  h. neither
  i. 0
  j. equal to
  k. fail
  l. the U.K. to the U.S.
  m. increase
  n. reduce

2*a.* higher
  b. fewer
  c. more
  d. rose
  e. depreciated
  f. decreased
  g. increased
  h. appreciation
  i. more
  j. less
  k. less
  l. more
  m. less